BUNTERS BREXIT

by

Paul Templeman

Illustrated by Andrew Fyfe

Any resemblance to former Prime-Ministers
alive or dead in a ditch is purely coincidental.

Contents

Chapter One

OUTSIDE THE DOOR of Number 10 cameras had been primed and pointed at an empty podium for twenty-two minutes. Commentators were making lame excuses in more than twenty languages and researchers trawled the Internet for increasingly obscure statistics to share about past Prime Ministers. Rain threatened and had become a convenient talking point for the world's broadcasters.

'You join us outside Downing Street, where the skies are overcast and rain threatens. If it begins to rain, will they move the press conference inside? Let's head back to the studio for detailed projections on the weather prospects.'

The press muttered and moaned and adjusted exposures and tripods. William George Bunter, newly elected Conservative Prime Minister of the United Kingdom was late for the speech that was intended to mark the pinnacle of his career. The world held its breath as dark storm clouds gathered overhead.

Rain had still failed to materialise when at last a familiar fat figure emerged with a diffident grin from the lacquered door of Number 10. His hair was newly ruffled, and there would afterwards be speculation about stains in the crotch of his suit. But there he was, as he always knew he would be…

'Now listen up you chaps!' he said, taking the podium.

'Well, crikey, who'd have thought it? I've just been to see Her Majesty the Queen who's invited me to form a government and I've— well, of course I've been minded to accept. Who wouldn't be so minded?

'So, here's the bit where I pay tribute to the unrecognised but quite exceptional talents of my predecessor, and her debatable sense of public service. A woman, you remember. Of course, if there were any justice, she would never have been given the job in the first place.

'My view - the public's view, let's be honest – she made a bit of a hash of it. Easy to say in retrospect. But naysayers since 2016 here and abroad seem to share her view that we can't honour ... well, we can't seem to honour a basic democratic mandate. So here I am today to tell you—the British people—that all those critics are wrong. I can honour it and I'll jolly well deliver it. I'll show you. And them.

'And all those blinkering, blathering, burbling Bandersnatches— they're about to choke on their tuck. Just you watch.

'The people who bet against Britain – they're going to lose their shirts because we're coming out of the EU on October 31 - no ifs, no buts as somebody once said. And we'll do a new deal. A better deal. And then Global Britain will go out there into the wider world and find new chums all over the world to trade with ... lots and lots of countries, many of which I've personally visited, and some of which I've never heard. But that doesn't matter.

'Remember, I have a record,' he grinned broadly and wagged a finger, 'not that kind of record, but a demonstrable record of success. And when Londoners called upon me to rescue their city from the destitution and despair caused by Marxism, I stepped up and transformed that place of dark satanic mills into the modern, thriving metropolis you see today. The most successful city in the world, with more police officers, more hospitals, less crime and less sick people than any place on earth. They said it wasn't possible.

'So, in 99 days' time exactly we'll have cracked it. That's what I'm asking of you: just 99 days. Put it in your diary if you have one. Set your watches. Together we'll get Brexit done!

'The Queen, whom I've just met, and whom I found to be happy, glorious, and not to say a victorious lady, has honoured me with this extraordinary office of state. But I want you to know that since my days at Greyfriars and Oxford I've always known this moment would arrive. The success of this country will be played out on the playing fields of Greyfriars. Its future has been debated and concluded in the cloisters of Oxford.

'From today I'm going to appoint a new government. A better one. A world-beating government. I've got a chum from Greyfriars who went to work in a bank after Oxford, and he'll make the most excellent chancellor. I've got other talented chums, too. A stable of them. It'll be a government of all the talents - the very best of Greyfriars's scholars. And other people.

'We start recruiting forthwith.

'In the future there'll be no need for anyone to visit the tuckshop – I intend to bring the tuck to the nation.

'And I'll tell you something else about my job.

'It's to be Prime Minister of the whole United Kingdom - and that means all of you out there in places I've never heard of - even if you don't have a penny to your name. Even if you're not white. Even if you're not heterosexual. I will be your Prime Minister. The chosen one. The one that will give you what every one of you told us you wanted: Brexit.

'We'll come out of the EU on October 31, just like I said we would. No ifs. No buts. It's my promise to you as a gentleman. And what's more, as your Prime Minister.

'Because in the end Brexit was a fundamental decision by the British people. It was your choice. People wanted their laws made by people they can elect and they can remove from office, and I'm it. Or at least I'm one of them. And we must now respect that decision.

'My old form at Greyfriars was called the Remove. I was nicknamed the Owl of the Remove, because I was wise and thoughtful. Now I like to think of myself as Head Remover – as we remove ourselves from the manacles of EU bureaucracy.

'We'll create a new partnership with our European friends – as warm and as close and as affectionate as possible, in the spirit of Churchill.

'And the first step is to get shot of all the EU nationals who are here already. And I say to them – thank you for your contribution to our society. Thanks – but no thanks. We don't need Johnny Foreigner making and mending things we don't want made or mended.

'Under this government you'll get the absolute certainty of the rights to leave as quickly as you want. And we'll help you with that. We'll support you.

'Next, I say to our friends in Ireland, and in Brussels and around the EU, I'm convinced we can do a deal without checks at the Irish border, because we refuse under any circumstances to have such checks. We'll cobble together some kind of deal between us, and we may need to sort out all the details later. And if not – if you are ever asked for paperwork to cross that border – call me. Call your Prime Minister. And I'll tell them what to do with their paperwork. Because I won't have it. I. Won't. Have. It. Because we're British. And Britons shall not ever be slaves.

'We may even build a bridge to Ireland as a showcase of British engineering. Like the garden bridge I built in London - plush with the indigenous flora and fauna of our nation. Except that this one would be much bigger and without the plants.

'Even so, it's vital to prepare for the minuscule possibility that Brussels will begrudge us our rightful freedom and we'll be forced to come out with no deal. We'll still have that 39 billion quid. Which buys a lot of tuck, I can tell you.

'And we'll be prepared for that day, just like boy scouts.

'The ports will be ready and the banks will be ready and the factories will be ready and businesses will be ready and the hospitals will be ready and our amazing food and farming sector will be ready and waiting to continue selling more than ever, not just here but around the globe.

'I'm not going to pretend that everything is going to be plain sailing. But we'll fight them on the beaches. In the tradition of Empire. Because we're British and we will overcome.

'So, beware: Never underestimate our powers of organisation and our determination, like the Germans did in 1939. And the Argentinians.

'I will lead this country to recover our natural and historic role as an enterprising, outward-looking and truly global Britain, generous in temper and engaged with the world.

'No one in the last few centuries has succeeded in betting against the pluck and nerve and ambition of this country. And they're not going to start now.

'I'm going to work flat out to give this country the leadership it deserves. Except at weekends and when I'm at Chequers. Even if it makes me sick. I'm jolly well starting right now.

'And I'm reminded of our school motto '*Conamur Tenues Grandia*': 'Though slight, we strive for greatness'. He paused and looked around at his audience. 'Which has always meant to me that the ant really CAN move that rubber tree plant—and I can! Thank you very much.'

'Prime Minister!' Yelled the press pack. 'Mr Bunter!'

Flashes flashed and shutters wooshed. Bunter waved as he disappeared inside Number 10 without looking back.

The heavens opened and a torrent of rain descended, just as the door of Number 10 closed. For the networks it was back to the studio for a report on the latest weather.

Chapter Two

BUNTER HAD HIS feet up on the desk. It put him in mind of his days in the Rag, the juniors' common room at Greyfriars School—the school that had nurtured him and shaped him. They had been happy days apart from the beatings and the bullying, he reflected. Sometimes he wasn't sure if his memories were half-remembered or half forgotten. And here before him as he reclined in the seat of power, was a fragment of those memories—his old chum, Bob Cherry, looking unaccountably miserable and of course decades older.

'I see you in Health,' said Bunter, brushing away the crumbs of a recently consumed pork pie.

'In good health, I trust?' replied Cherry, looking anything but.

'I meant Secretary of State for Health.'

Cherry shifted in his seat. 'Seems like that might be hard work. And I rather like the sheer indolence of being an MP.'

'Nonsense. And there's a fortune to be made for a shrewd operator. Which you are.'

'Why?'

'Why are you a shrewd operator?'

'No. Why would you appoint me as Health Secretary?' said Cherry.

Bunter tapped the side of his nose. 'Because you are a person as never forgets who put him where he is.'

Cherry looked blank. 'Meaning?'

'Do I have to spell it out? The NHS is a very big pie. Ripe for slicing up. Deals to be done.'

'Is that a bow tie you're wearing, Bunter?'

Bunter preened himself, tugging at a blue and white spotted bow. 'Like it?'

'Is it a new image?'

'Indeed, old chap. How's your father, the Major? A school governor wasn't he?'

'He died in 1976.'

Bunter's exuberance faltered. 'Sorry to hear that old chap. Was it sudden?'

'I'm over it now, Bunter. It was over 40 years ago.'

'Still…'

Cherry stood up. 'I'll think about Health.'

Bunter scrambled to his feet. He was taller than Cherry by six inches, and more than twice as wide.

'Do more than think about it, if you don't mind. I've got to fill all these jobs by lunchtime,' grumbled Bunter. 'Todd gave me a list—can you believe Todd is Cabinet Secretary?—and it's very nearly 10 o'clock.'

'Peter Todd from school?'

'The very same,' said Bunter, beaming. He was always jolly decent to me, not like the rest of you beastly lot.' Bunter accompanied Cherry to the door and laid a hand on his back as though to hustle him out of the room. 'The nation's health is in your hands, old chap.'

'Not yet it isn't,' said Cherry.

Out in the ante-room Huree Jamset Ram Singh stood up, nodding to Cherry who rolled his eyes as he left. Bunter's secretary also stood up and Bunter noticed with approval that her skirt was shorter than yesterday.

'Is it OK to let him through, Prime Minister?'

'Of course, of course.' Bunter extended a fat hand. 'Inky! Old chap. So good to see you.'

'Bunter,' said Singh with a sour look, allowing his hand to be grasped. 'Many felicitations on your most esteemed appointment.'

Bunter grinned. 'Good show, isn't it? Come into my parlour.' Singh followed Bunter into the csavernous office, where Bunter busied himself at a cocktail cabinet and slopped red wine into a glass. 'Drink, old chap? Look, they have everything. Whisky, gin.. Not even locked up.'

'I don't...' said Singh.

'No. Of course not. You don't need to tell me about the religious privations of your tribe.'

'I mean I don't, at this time of the morning.'

Bunter established himself behind his desk and propped up his legs, knocking an important looking red box to the floor.

'Is it a bow tie you're wearing, Bunter?'

'Do you like it?'

'Superbly Churchillian.'

'Do you think so?' said Bunter with an uncertain note. Singh had always been the clever one. It was hard to know when he was sincere.

'To what purpose am I summoned to your great office?' he said, looking around him. 'The shabbiness is rather more than one would have anticipated.'

'Looks fine to me,' said Bunter, casting a worrisome look around the room. 'That aside, Inky, what do you think? I have to put together a cabinet of the great and the good. And when I learned you were an MP – well we've always been the very best of friends..'

'It is not forgotten that you remain indebted to me in the sum of 6 shillings.'

'Indeed, indeed. And it's your pecuniary wizardry that made me think of you.'

'Oh?'

Bunter gulped at his wine, swung his legs from the desk and bunched his meaty shoulders as he leaned towards Singh in a confiding manner.

'How would you like to be Chancellor?'

Singh looked less enthused that Bunter had hoped. 'Will it cost me anything?'

Bunter laughed. 'Why would it cost you anything?'

'I fondly remember my time at the Greyfriars establishment and my many dealings with the Owl of the Remove as you once were. I seem to remember at each encounter it was I that emerged the poorer.'

Bunter laughed. 'The Owl? Nobody's called me that in many years, old boy. Good gracious,' said Bunter, at once dipping into his pocket. 'You know I always repay my debts, no matter how trifling. How much is six shillings in today's money? Thirty pence? I'll pay you now with interest.'

'Really, there is no needfulness.'

Bunter fumbled in his jacket. 'I insist.' He fumbled some more but his hand emerged empty. I'll have to owe you.'

'Really, Bunter. Don't trouble yourself,' said Singh.

'Very well. So how about it? Chancellor, what?'

'I shall undertake to give it my full consideration.'

'Cherry's got Health.'

'His healthfulness was supremely evident when I saw him.'

'I mean he's agreed to be Health Secretary. It'll be like old times.'

Singh looked doubtful. 'I see.'

'So, I can count on you?'

'The position of chancellor will indeed require much counting.'

As Bunter showed him to the door, he said: 'Wasn't your father a bus driver, Inky?'

'He is the proprietor and owner of East Coast Railways. And an airline.'

'Knew it was something like that. You should make more of your humble origins, you know. The public like that kind of thing. Well let me know. Cabinet meeting in the morning, 8:30 sharpish. Debbie?' He summoned his secretary.

'My name is Mandy, Prime Minister.'

'So sorry, Mandy. Please see Mr Singh out.'

Bunter was having enormous fun. In assembling his Cabinet he felt as though he were settling old scores, as well as impressing on everyone his importance and his magnitude. Dutton was next and Mandy showed him into Bunter's office with a flourish of her manicured nails and a waft of perfume.

'Mr Thomas Dutton, Prime Minister.'

'Tom!' Exclaimed Bunter, leaping up as quickly as his bountiful frame would allow and giving Dutton an entirely unexpected bear hug. 'My old chum,' said Bunter.

Dutton flinched and allowed himself to be patted on the back by Bunter with some misgiving.

'Delighted to see you again old chap,' said Dutton without enthusiasm, narrowing his thorny eyebrows.

Bunter released him and Dutton breathed a sigh.

'Drink?' said Bunter.

Dutton sniffed the air. 'Can't smell anything, old boy.' Dutton was afflicted with deafness, a trait shared by many MPs.

'Not stink. Drink. I said: would you like a drink, old man?'

'No need to shout. I'm not as deaf as you think.'

'So, what's it to be?'

Dutton looked at the cocktail cabinet with lust. 'Large Scotch.'

'On the rocks?'

'Eh? What?'

'With ice?'

Dutton looked around the office, into the corners and along the threshold. 'These old buildings. You can't keep 'em out.'

'Keep what out, old chap?'

'Mice. Little blighters.'

'I said ice.'

'Best thing is to lay down poison. We have poison everywhere at Dutton Hall y'know.'

Bunter handed him his drink and Dutton swallowed it in one, then held out his glass. 'Don't mind if I do. A trifle parched,' then he seated himself in front of the fireplace, in a cracked leather armchair and seemed to nod off.

Bunter settled down opposite and tapped him on the knee. 'You can't sleep here you know.'

Dutton spluttered and shook himself awake. 'Is there a Division?'

'You're not in the House.'

'Mouse? Little blighters. Didn't I tell you to lay down poison? That's the ticket.'

'How would you like to be Justice Secretary?'

'Sorry old boy. I've got one.'

'Got what?'

'A secretary. Can't just boot her out, y'know.'

Bunter raised his voice. 'Justice Secretary. How would you like to be Justice Secretary?'

'If it's all right with you, it's all right with me. Thought justice was meant to be blind, not deaf.' He spluttered at his own joke, shook his jowls and presented his glass again. 'Any more where this came from or should we start on the good stuff, eh?'

Bunter hitched up his trousers and surveyed the expectant faces in the ante-room. He almost didn't recognise the newly hirsute Wharton in a

Wodehousian check suit. He looked at his watch. Lunch was beckoning across the hours. He pointed. 'Wharton. Foreign Secretary.'

Wharton brightened. 'Thank you, Prime Minister.'

'Think nothing of it, old chap.'

A beaky nosed woman with a Thatcher perm complained: '*Must* one be a Greyfriars Old Boy to be in the Cabinet?'

Bunter pondered. The word diversity came to mind. The most diverse Cabinet in history. World-beating diversity, in fact. He liked the idea of that. 'Who might you be?'

'I am Penelope Portmanteau, Member for PontyPryd.'

'School?'

'Marlborough.'

'Culture Secretary,' decided Bunter at once.

A grey, gaunt man in round spectacles languished on a couch and seemed to exude monochrome. Bunter thought he recalled him from Oxford. He wagged a finger. 'Don't I know you?'

'Sir Oliver Tempus-Fugitson. We were at Pembroke,' he drawled, without much interest. The monochrome seemed to have seeped into the couch, which was no longer green but grey. 'Also at Greyfriars but you were just a tadpole then.'

'Secretary for the Nineteenth Century.'

'Does that even exist?' Protested a man crowned with an improbable wig.

'It does now. We're going to exploit the achievements of the Victorians, and Tempus-Fugitson is the very man to do it.'

'But you can't just invent ministerial portfolios!'

Bunter raised himself up on his toes. 'Am I not the Prime Minister? Surely, I can do anything I please.'

'When you put it like that,' said Johnny Bull, another Greyfriars Old Boy.

Bunter gestured at Bull 'Levelling Up Secretary,' he pronounced, the role having just occurred to him.

'What does that mean?' said Bull

'We'll think of something, I expect. But now - to deliver on my gold-plated election promise. Whom shall I appoint as Brexit Secretary?'

Everyone in the room became suddenly occupied with their mobile phones, reading or replying to messages. Bunter looked for a victim and found Jeremy Truscott.

'Truscott, old chap. It's you isn't it? You were in the Bounders Club at Oxford.'

'I was that.'

'As an Old Bounder you will make an excellent Brexit Secretary. You're just the man to get Brexit done.'

'But I voted Remain.'

'Even better. What the public wants to see is reformed Remainers delivering our dream.'

'More of a nightmare. That's why I voted against it. Think about the lost trade, the lack of free movement, the added bureacrasy…'

'But you'll do it?' interrupted Bunter with impatience.

Truscott considered.

'Probably a 'K' in it for you and you'll be in the Cabinet.'

'Wouldn't miss it for the world.'

'That's the spirit, old chap.'

Chapter Three

IN THE CORRIDOR on the way to his first Cabinet meeting, Bunter was in buoyant mood. He encountered a familiar figure, stooping and striding briskly towards him who looked up and fixed Bunter with a gimlet eye, undiminished by the last 35 years.

'Quelch!' said Bunter in alarm.

Quelch glared. '*Lord* Quelch to you, Bunter.'

'What are you doing here?'

'I Chair the Privileges Committee.'

'How did you get in? I mean, how did you get a peerage?'

'Services to the state, Bunter. Something about which you probably know little if I'm a judge. Which I'm not. Lacking the legal qualifications, d'you see?'

'Harsh, sir. I've always done my best.'

Quelch seemed to draw himself up and Bunter recoiled. A disturbing memory came to mind of Quelch, cane uplifted, face crimson with fury.

'I've followed your career closely since Greyfriars, Bunter.'

'Glad to hear it, sir. I mean ter say Lord Quelch.'

'I've got my eye on you.'

'I haven't done anything.'

'Exactly!' Barked Quelch. 'You've done precisely nothing to merit elevation to this great office.'

Bunter opened his hands to indicate he was not responsible. 'I never sought high office. But my public and the Conservative Party put me here.'

'I saw you in that TV interview.'

'Which one?'

"'A nasty piece of work." That's what he called you.'

Bunter's face dropped. 'You mean that one.'

'That journalist. You know the one. Mrs Q and I were in stitches. He had you bang to rights, as it were.' Quelch chuckled at the memory. He raised a bony finger in the air like he used to in class when emphasising a salient point. 'I'll be keeping an eye on you, Bunter,' and he marched away, oblivious to the civil servants and MPs stepping aside for him.

'Oh Cripes,' thought Bunter.

A paper dart wafted gently through the air, executed a spin and then slid along the boardroom table to settle directly in front of Bunter. With a grim smile, Bunter screwed it into a ball and directed it at Dutton, who appeared to be sleeping.

'Oi! I heard that. What?' spluttered Dutton. He half got to his feet and then sat down again.

The general hubbub died away. Someone may have farted, but it was hard to be sure in the humid sweat-tinged atmosphere. Bunter, hunched halfway down the table squeezed between Singh and Mauly, called the meeting to order.

'Good morning one and all. I take uncommon delight in welcoming this new team reflecting the depth and breadth of our most glorious party. You are all part of my Cabinet for Modern Britain and together we shall embark on a momentous journey, the likes of which this country has never seen. We are all of us committed to leaving the EU on the 31 October. If not before. No if, no buts, just as I told the public in my speech.'

There ensued a thumping on the table which roused Truscott, who at once bellowed 'Hear, hear!' before descending again into an apparent slumber.

Truscott raised a hand to speak. 'But..' He began.

'Didn't you hear me, old chap? I said no ifs, no buts. It's *sine qua non*. Our mission is to Get Brexit Done - and I intend for this proud nation to prosper mightily during my tenure. To prosper mightily,' he repeated to a patter of softer thumps on the table. He searched for his place in a red binder, running a finger down the page. His lips moved silently before he added: 'Indeed we will. I've invited along to this meeting my Special Parliamentary Advisor Gregory Kaminsky who you may remember played a key role in the campaign to rid ourselves of the shackles of EU bureaucracy. Erm, Gregory..? Would you say a few words, old boy?' Bunter waved a careless hand in the direction of a shaven headed man in a track suit sitting along the periphery of the room, leaning with his elbows on his knees. He looked up.

'Morning everyone.' Kaminsky spoke with a Northern burr that seemed to rattle the tea cups. 'The Prime Minister's asked me to step in and help shape the nature of our departure from the EU.'

'Isn't Kaminsky a Russian name?' said Cherry.

'I was born in Durham.'

'But your lineage - is that Russian?'

'My middle name is Edward.'

'So, you're not Russian?'

'There's no question about my commitment to the prosperity of the United Kingdom.'

'I wasn't questioning your commitment...'

Bunter interrupted. 'There it is chaps. I think we can all be reassured that there's no question about Gregory's commitment, integrity or faithful endeavour when it comes to this great nation - one which I fully intend to make even greater and more prosperous—you see if I don't. And I'll hear no more about it.'

'Spasibo, Prime Minister,' said Kaminsky concealing a smirk behind a forefinger.

Sir Tempus-Fugitson's monochrome aura had drained his neighbours of colour and was extending to Kaminsky from his place at the table. He spoke up in a pompous tone: 'I postulate that I may assist Mr Kaminsky in capitalising some of the benefits from our Victorian age that have been stifled by the inglorious European Union.'

Kaminsky grunted. 'Ruddy toffs.'

'What?'

'I said that would be really great.'

'Next item on the agenda,' said Bunter, 'Downing Street parties. You're all invited, but it's strictly BYOB.'

Murmurs of 'Thank you, Prime Minister.'

Bunter noticed the diminutive Rajmar Pandit for the first time, just across the table. He frowned. What are you doing here, Rajmar?'

'You appointed me Home Secretary, Prime Minister.'

'Did I? Crikey. I think there may have been a misunderstanding. I think what I said was that you may make someone a fine secretary one day.'

'I'm an MP.'

'Good gracious. Who'd have thought it?' said Bunter in wonder. 'Where is your constituency?'

'Woestable and Battering.'

'I haven't the foggiest where that is.'

'Well.. I'm here now,' said Pandit in discomfort.

'So you are. Jolly good too! Well.. welcome to government. Never let it be said that I am not building a diverse government. Now..' He shuffled his papers, but then as an afterthought looked back at Pandit. 'Is that an actual uniform you're wearing, Rajmar?'

She shifted in her seat. 'I think it just looks that way, Prime Minister. Because it's black. And, you know, with the silver buttons.'

'Hmmm. Yes. Suits you,' he turned to the rest of the table, 'First thing on the agenda is trade deals. My chum Fisher T Fisher, the US President, has promised me the most spectacular US trade deal..' He scowled suddenly at an empty chair. 'Where's the Trade Secretary?'

'Lost, Prime Minister,' said Cherry.

Kaminsky tutted.

'Lost!?'

'She sent me a text,' said Cherry. 'It's her first Cabinet meeting, and this place is a bit of a labyrinth if you're not used to it.'

'What did she say.'

Cherry squinted at his screen and read the text: 'Soz. Lost in corridors of power. Laters.'

'Soz?'

'It means...'

'I know what it means!'

The door opened and Gloria Pendlesham sidled in. 'Sorry,' she mouthed, and took a vacant seat.

'I should jolly well hope so.'

'Idiot.' Muttered Kaminsky, almost beneath his breath but loud enough for the whole room to hear clearly.

'We were talking about America,' said Bunter.

Pendlesham brightened at once. 'I've been there.' She looked at Pandit for support. 'Disney Land,' she clarified. 'With George and the kids.'

'Enlightening as it may be to hear about Mickey Mouse, Gloria...'

'MOUSE!' thundered Dutton, suddenly alert. 'Blighters! Don't worry. Poison's the answer. I was telling wattsisname…'

Singh nudged him. 'The lackfulness of mice is beyond question,' he said in a low voice.

'Only yesterday,' Bunter resumed, 'I was on the blower to my good chum Donald. And I want you, Gloria, to hop on the Prime Ministerial jet and go and get our first trade deal signed.'

'Do we have a Prime-ministerial jet?' Said Pendlesham.

Bunter waved a dismissive hand. 'If we don't we'll jolly well charter one. Now... To the next item. Whom did I make Health Secretary?'

Cherry spoke up. 'That'll be me. Although I haven't really decided yet. I just thought I'd drop in and see what happens at Cabinet meetings. Can we chat about the NHS budget?

'Budgets are Inky's remit,' directing his thumb at Singh, who looked uncomfortable.

'Yes, but specifically - about the £350 million a week we'll be saving from the EU,' said Cherry.

Bunter looked around the table, reading the room. 'That was, erm.. Figurative, old chap.'

'Figurative?'

'Of course. It's about figures, isn't it? Remember I studied classics not maths, old boy. I'm not to know...'

'It was on the side of your campaign bus. That big red Leave campaign bus.'

'You can't believe everything you read on the side of a bus. Sometimes not even the destination is truthful. D'you know, I was on a bus once...'

'But you said we sent £350 million per week to the EU..'

'Yes but not consecutively.'

'What?'

Bunter sighed with impatience. 'Not on consecutive weeks. Sometimes they would send us money. Anyway it wasn't me - it was Gregory.'

Everyone turned to Kaminsky.

'Of course it was me,' growled Kaminsky.

'And where did the figure come from?' said Cherry.

'I made it up.'

There was a stunned silence as the Cabinet absorbed this.

'We won, didn't we?' said Kaminsky in an abrasive, challenging tone.

'Gregory has a point.' said Bunter. 'Anyway, what's done is done and I was clearly not to blame. For anything. Until just now for instance I didn't know that Gregory had made it up. Not even what the exact figure was. I most definitely was not to blame.'

Cherry shook his head in despair. 'You never were, were you? I remember that from Greyfriars.'

'Because it was true. And Gregory's right: we won, didn't we?'

'I told you all about it, you old fraud,' said Kaminsky to himself.

Bunter glared at him. 'I won't have division in the Cabinet..'

Dutton leapt to his feet. 'Division!' he bellowed. 'Division! Don't dawdle. We need to vote at once,' and he made for the door, leaning for support on the backs of chairs as he went.

Cherry tapped his temple.

'Sit down Dutton,' said Bunter.

'What's that old bean?'

'SIT!'

Dutton returned to his seat, mumbling. 'There used to be bells for divisions,' he muttered, 'place has gone to hell in a handcart.'

Bunter allowed calm to settle and then pronounced in a mellifluous tone, and with an air of finality: '*Aeì ho theòs geōmetreî.*'

'What?' said Cherry.

'It's Greek,' said Bunter with pride.

'I know it's Greek,' said Cherry, 'but what does it mean?'

'It's famous. Everybody knows … Socrates.'

'Plato,' interjected Tempus-Fugitson, folding his hands on the table and shuffling on his chair in monochrome ecstasy.

'Whoever said it is immaterial. I asked what it meant?' said Cherry.

Bunter's demonstration of his classical education was wearing thin. 'It's just a figure of speech. A closing thought,' he said, floundering.

'Something to do with geometry I shouldn't wonder,' hazarded Dutton, as though the very idea of mathematics might be black magic.

'Can we stop talking about the Greeks?' said Kaminsky.

'What have the Greeks ever done to us?' said Cherry.

'Don't they want their marbles back?' said Pendlesham.

Bunter beamed around the table. 'Questions anyone?'

Bunter was bathing in the afterglow of his success. He was living the dream. King of kings. He sipped at his red wine and slouched in the pumped-up sofa. He liked Number 11. He liked its simple ambience much more than the stuffy decor at Number 10 that so reminded him of Bunter Court. He munched on a ham roll and the mustard made his head swim…

Marianne crossed her long legs and brushed back a ringlet. 'This John Lewis crap will have to go. It's hideous,' she said, surveying the room as she rested the rim of her glass of Puglio against a plump lower lip. She glared at Bunter from across the John Lewis coffee table.

'Yes. I rather thought that too, Piglet. Detestable.'

'And don't call me Piglet in front of the staff again.'

'Sorry. Slip of the tongue, Piglet.'

She recrossed her legs. 'We'll have to redecorate. I can't abide it.'

'Of course, Piglet. But I'm on a Prime Minister's salary now. We can't go crazy y'know.'

'Somebody can pay for it. Anybody can pay for it. There are plenty of donors. What about Lord whatsisname? He's always giving you money.'

'Dovecote?'

'That's the one.'

'I'll talk to him. But I wouldn't mention it to anyone. About the money. After all he doesn't give me money. And if he did it would be quite legitimate. I spent it on electioneering. That's if he gave me any, which he didn't.' Bunter became flustered.

'Never mind that now. There's something else.'

'Yes, Piglet,' he said, with a rising sense of foreboding.

'We'll have to get married.'

Bunter coughed up some crumbs. 'But whatever for?'

'I'm an ambitious woman, Billy. You knew that when you met me.'

'Yes, but..'

'I can't play second fiddle to you all my life.'

'You're the wife of the Prime Minister!'

'Maybe I want to be Prime Minister, one day.'

'You..?'

'You're not a young man, Billy. Look at Hilary Clinton.'

'Hilary Clinton,' he repeated slowly.

'Do you think she could have been a Presidential Candidate if she'd just been Bill's floozy?' She sipped at her wine and giggled suddenly. 'He's got the same name as you, Billy.'

'Yes. Yes he does.'

Marianne's eyes misted over. 'I want to create a Bunter dynasty,' she said.

'O lor,' said Bunter.

Chapter Four

THE ROOM BUMPED and shifted and loud music bounced off the walls. A naked girl was dancing in a mirror except there didn't seem to be a mirror. Twins, Bunter realised with delight, and they were writhing and grinding against each other, blonde hair flailing. He sipped his Champagne, which he almost spilt when somebody clapped a heavy hand on his back.

'There you are!' said Ignatov loudly in his ear. 'Enjoying the party?'

It was Ignatov's party - his fiftieth birthday party, except that he looked younger. Bunter wondered if he died his thick, black beard.

'One of your best, Iggy old chap.' He had to shout over the music, but still Ignatov cupped a hand over his ear.

'What's that?' He beckoned. 'Come and meet father.'

Bunter allowed himself to be steered though the crowded room and into a long hallway lined with ancient portraits.

'These your ancestors, Sasha?'

Ignatov laughed. 'Came with the chateau. No idea who they are. They might be ancestors, come to think of it.'

A familiar hulking pot-bellied man with a pudding-basin haircut passed them in the corridor dragging a waif of a girl in a floaty almost transparent dress into a side room. She had a high forehead and a pencil thin waist and was giggling and bubbling uncontrollably leaving a trail of Champagne in her wake on the tiled floor. The hulking man seemed to wink at Bunter. He displayed sharp incisors when he smiled.

'I say,' said Bunter to Ignatov, 'Wasn't that the Duke of Yorkshire?'

'What happens in Umbria, stays in Umbria,' said Ignatov with a sly look. 'Come on, father's waiting.'

'I've never met your father.'

'You're about to,' he said, pushing open a heavy oak door. 'He's very keen to meet you.'

Ignatov's father was standing with his back to a row of French windows that opened onto a perfect emerald lawn. He was rugged and angular and had a twisted nose. His black tie dangled unfastened. He came up to Bunter at once and threw his arms around him in an iron embrace.

'What a pleasure!' he exclaimed, and kissed Bunter hard on the lips. Bunter tried to recoil but the grip was firm.

'Meet my father, Alexei.'

Alexei grinned and released him. 'You can call me Volk. Everyone does this. It means Wolf,' he said, with a thick Russian slur.

Dazed and unsteady after Volk's greeting, Bunter said 'Why do they call you that?'

Volk frowned. 'Fucked if I know,' he growled. He glanced at the door though which Bunter had entered. 'Any trouble?'

'Trouble?'

'With security.'

'What security?'

'Your security. Man of your position. MI5? MI6? I can't keep up,' he waved a dismissive hand.

'Father was KGB.' Ignatov clarified.

'Lost them at the airport,' said Bunter with pride. 'It wasn't hard.'

'Can't be too careful,' said Volk, glancing around the room as if he expected somebody to emerge from behind a curtain or under a table. 'Let's talk outside.'

'I'll leave you two to talk,' said Ignatov, eager to get back to his party.

'Alright, old chap. I'll be fine with Volk.'

Volk winked at him. 'We understand each other, yes?'

In the garden, Volk walked briskly with his hands behind his back. The sun was going down. Music drifted in the air. Bunter made an effort to keep up. They reached a gazebo with a fountain, out of sight of the house and surrounded by shrubs, at least one of which Bunter recognised. Volk sat down and planted a meaty hand on Bunter's thigh. 'I wanted for us to have a conversation about the election,' he said.

'What election?' Said Bunter.

'The one you're going to have before Christmas.'

'But I've only just become Prime Minister.'

'Impossible to deliver our agenda—that is, YOUR agenda—with minority government. I think this is axiomatic, yes?'

'But I hadn't planned...'

'No need to worry. You won't need to plan. We will take care of everything. Gregor will do it.'

Bunter had a creeping unease. 'But what if I lose?'

Volk laughed. 'Losing is not convenient option.' He patted Bunter's knee. 'There will be no talk of losing, my friend. Look,' he rose to his feet with a smile that was almost a grimace, wiping his palm on the leg of his trousers. 'Somebody I wish you to meet.'

Bunter stood up to greet an outsize, flowery woman with starched curls that brought to mind rusty springs and a wide purple crease where her smile should have been.

'This,' announced Volk, taking her hand, 'Is Irina Malenkova. Maybe you know about her?'

Bunter was quick to take her hand, which was hot and damp. 'A pleasure, Irina.'

'Pryatno Poznokomitsya!'

Bunter looked at Volk, who shook his head. 'She speaks no English.'

'Nothing speak,' said Irina in confirmation with a helpless gesture, shaking her starched curls.

'Irina is biggest donor to Conservative Party.'

'That's wonderful!' said Bunter, grinning and nodding at Irina and wondering how long he was expected to suffer her. 'I didn't know that.'

'Details,' said Volk. 'Biggest donor in history of your party. Bigger maybe, nobody can tell because Irina, she gives nothing directly. Just through offshore companies.'

Irina was smiling, but seemed bewildered. She muttered

something in Russian to Volk and when he answered she nodded. 'Yes, yes!' she said with enthusiasm.

'She has donated already 32 million of your British pounds. She is very wealthy lady.'

'I am so, so grateful to you,' said Bunter gratefully, making a big effort to be sincere, and forgetting that he was still holding her hand. She tugged it away and said something to Volk.

'Irina say she is much admiring of your Brexit.'

'Wonderful.' Bunter repeated, nodding at Irina who nodded back.

'Thank you and bye,' she said with an abrupt wave and a glance at Volk.

Volk turned to Bunter. 'And now you can get back to your twins.'

'How did you..?'

Volk slapped him hard on the back and guffawed. 'I was KGB officer, you know? In London even. I was paid to know about what is going on.' He put a heavy hand on Bunter's shoulder and leant in. Bunter hoped he wouldn't kiss him again. He could smell alcohol and cigars 'Some word of advice,' he said in a low voice. 'Look out for cameras.'

'Cameras?'

Volk straightened up. 'Don't be like Fisher T Fisher. Still we laugh about those pissing videos.'

Bunter thought for an instant. 'So these twins..?'

'All yours, Billy my friend. Just be careful.'

Bunter was snoozing in a crumpled suit on a plastic chair. Sometimes he slipped sideways and corrected himself with a start—this was hardly unprecedented behaviour. He felt warm and safe here. A tinny voice announced a flight to Manchester, which was not where he wanted to go, so he slumbered on. When he began to collapse to one side he stirred. His eyes were sticky. On his lap he was nursing a duty-free bag, its contents a mystery. People swirled around him wheeling luggage which rattled painfully in his head. A man and a woman were seated on either side of him, leaning in to take a selfie.

'What do you think you're doing?' spluttered Bunter in righteous indignation.

Oblivious, a shovel faced man in his fifties remarked to his wife: 'Man of the people. That's what I've always said about Billy,'

'You always said that, Frank. You always did,' said the woman sitting to Bunter's left. She was grey and plump and stoic, wearing a 'T' shirt that professed her love for Milan, and serving to emphasise her rolls of flesh.

Bunter looked from one to the other and blinked.

''S why he'll always have my support,' said the man in a sage tone.

'He'll always have our support, Frank. That's what you always say.' She addressed Bunter directly for the first time: 'That's what my Derek always says,' she said with a sage nod.

'Thick and thin. That's what I always say,' said Derek, beaming with munificence.

'You've always said it, Frank. To your credit, you always have. They have to give you that, don't they: you've always said it.'

'Who are you people?' said Bunter, with undisguised distaste. Bunter detected the acrid smell of stale clothing and tobacco.

'We're Billy loyalists. Some of your biggest fans. Get Brexit Done,' said the man with a cracked laugh, displaying a thumbs up.'

'Yes. Get Brexit Done,' the woman echoed.

'Hashtag Back Billy,' said the man.

'That's nice,' said Bunter, looking about him in discomfort.

'You can always rely on our vote,' said Derek, patting Bunter on the shoulder and taking another selfie. Bunter shrank into his seat.

'You can rely on us, Mr Bunter, sir,' said his wife. 'No matter what that Beaver man says. Thick and thin.'

'Sorry, would you please give me some space. I think I'm likely throw up,' said Bunter. 'Oh golly, now what?' Two improbably large men in identical blazers were approaching. They looked like angry policemen.

'We're policemen, Mr Bunter. We've been looking for you,' said one.

'I'm Detective John Miles of SO1,' said the other, reaching inside his blazer. Bunter flinched, but all Miles produced was an ID card, which he flourished at Bunter and at Derek and his wife. He reached out towards Derek and snapped his fingers. 'I'm afraid I'll need to take that phone, sir. This is my colleague, Detective John Miles. Also of SO1.'

'You can't do that. It's a liberty,' complained Derek. 'Are you going to just let them take my phone, Billy?'

'So, you're both called John Miles?' said Derek's wife.

'It does cause confusion,' admitted one of the detectives.

'Wait,' said Bunter, 'This gentleman is quite right. You can't just walk up and take a fellow's phone. It's not right. It's not what we stand for. It's not what we fought the Nazis for.'

The detective showed Bunter the photographs on the phone.

'Ah, yes. Well that does look rather ... yes, well obviously the photos need to go.'

The detective swiped away the pictures, pausing first at each one with a rueful smile, then handed back the phone. 'Now, sir. We need to talk privately to Mr Bunter here.'

'Stood up for our rights, he did,' said Derek holding up his Samsung Galaxy. 'Straight off. A man of the people. Like I've always said.'

'Yes, sir. Now if you'd please move along,' prompted one of the Mileses.

Derek gave Bunter a thumbs up as he moved off, and his wife said: 'Get Brexit done!'

Bunter gave a thumbs up in return and turned to the police officers.

'Do you have any aspirin?' said Bunter in a weak voice. The policemen looked at each other. One shook his head.

'How did you give us the slip, sir?'

Bunter pointed at each of the policemen with a broad grin. 'Miles and Miles.'

'What about it?'

'After Brexit you'll need to be known as Kilometres and Kilometres.'

'Very funny, sir,' said one.

'Mind telling us where you've been, sir?' said the other Miles.

'You're not authorised...' began Bunter. 'I mean it's a state secret,' Bunter tapped the side of his nose. 'Anyway, I'm not saying a word. I didn't do anything, actually. And if I did, it has nothing to do with you. I'm the Prime Minister, you know.'

Chapter Five

BUNTER HAD HIS legs propped on his desk at Number 10 once again and was munching on a sausage roll. It was Friday. Wine Time Friday beckoned in the afternoon. He was blissful and lethargic.

'How was the party?' said Kaminsky. Today Kaminsky seemed to be dressed in military fatigues.

'Rather good, old boy. Iggy throws a splendid bash.' He thought he saw Kaminsky wink, but he may have been mistaken. 'There was an official aspect to the visit.'

'I don't want to know about that. Please don't tell me about that.,' said Kaminsky raising a constraining hand. 'So, I've been having some thoughts about the election,' said Kaminsky, all business.

'I haven't decided to have one yet,' said Bunter.

'With respect it's not really your decision.'

'I'm the Prime Minister.'

'Not for long, if you don't have an election.'

'What makes you think that?'

Kaminsky sucked through his teeth and shook his head slowly. 'You're running a shit show and it's a minority shit show. If you don't get Brexit done you'll be out on your ear. A vote of no confidence. Just like the last poor cow. To avoid that you'll need a majority, so at least you'll be able to govern with a majority shit show. Fortunately, you've got me and the donors to take care of it. Now, pay attention.'

Bunter removed his legs from the desk and sat up. Kaminsky always made him feel nervous.

Kaminsky swivelled his iPad around and showed Bunter a grotesque cartoon of James Beaver characterised as a large beaver bearing an EU flag, proudly standing with one foot mounted on the corpse of Britannia. The message emblazoned on it was: 'Beware the Beaver.'

'Our new campaign message,' said Kaminsky.

Bunter glanced at it. 'Colourful.'

'We need to portray the Labour leader as a threat. Particularly a threat to Brexit.'

'And is he? A threat?'

Kaminsky shrugged. 'It's a single-issue election and the Beaver doesn't know where he stands on it. He's facing 61 motions to revoke Article 50.'

'And what's Article 50?' said Bunter with gravity.

'It doesn't matter right now.'

'Isn't Beaver pro-Brexit?'

Kaminsky laughed. 'He vacillates. That's his problem. That's our problem, in fact. So, we need to dress him up as a raving fucking Remainer, deliberately standing in the way of the will of the public.'

Kaminsky swiped the screen and turned it again to face Bunter. There was an image of British soldiers in trenches. A Turkish flag flew from the opposite trench. The caption said: 'Churchill fought off the Turks in Gallipoli. Now they're joining the EU.'

'Didn't the Turks win at Gallipoli?'

'You can't expect the electorate to know that.'

'And would they do that? Would they really approve Turkish EU membership?'

'Not a fucking chance. Anyway the UK has a veto. But you can't expect the electorate to know shit.'

'So what can we expect the electorate to know?'

'Only what we tell them.'

'It's all about Brexit then?'

'It always was.'

Bunter coughed into his fist. 'I was a Remainer before. Did you know that?'

'I wouldn't mention that if I were you. The electorate won't know it.'

'I think I was pretty vocal at the time.'

'The past is another country.'

'Yes, it is rather, isn't it? Is that Shakespeare?'

'LG Hartley—from the Go Between, which is what I feel like, most of the time. Listen, the new manifesto is big on Getting Brexit Done. There's some extra shit about more police and nurses, but you don't need to worry about that. Kicking the immigrants out: that's what the public wants. British jobs for British workers.'

'And do we have enough of them? British workers?'

'That's not important.'

'The electorate won't know that?' said Bunter.

'Now you're getting it.'

There was a knock on the door and Mandy poked her plumed head around the door.

'I've got Lord Quelch on the line, Prime Minister.'

Bunter shuddered. 'Tell him I'm not in. And tell him if I was in I would be in a meeting. But I'm not in. Assuredly.'

Kaminsky raised an eyebrow.

'He keeps phoning me. About some report.'

'The Russia Report?'

'That's the one.'

'We may need to do something about that. By which I mean nothing.'

'So what does it actually say?'

'Nothing much. It's been redacted.'

'Can't I see it? The full report? After all, I'm the highest authority in the land.'

'The security services don't trust you.'

'I thought they worked for me!' said Bunter in umbrage.

'Not directly. Only yesterday for example you pissed them off. Losing them at the airport like that. How do you tell your boss you lost a 20 stone Prime Minister?'

'Well who then? Who do they work for, if not me?'

'It'll be in the report. In the abridged sections. You'll see.'

'I'd like to,' grumbled Bunter.

'I don't think anyone should see it. Or if they have to, only the abridged version. Redacted, of course.'

'Have you seen it?'

Kaminsky hesitated. 'I've got clearance.'

'Just a minute.. You're got clearance, but I haven't?'

'It's nothing personal.'

'How can it not be personal?' said Bunter, angry now.

'We've all got your best interests at heart, Billy.'

'I'm not happy about this.' He reached for another sausage roll. 'I mean what am I supposed to do?'

'Try not to take Quelch's calls. That's my advice.'

'I won't be at home for Quelch's calls. I'll make it my business. I'm used to evading Quelch. I remember once at school...' He rubbed his hands and the crumbs from his sausage roll fluttered in the air.

'Yes, yes. Let's not start on the Greyfriars reminiscences. We need to talk about the bill on Wednesday.'

'What bill would that be, old chap?'

'I like to call it the 'Surrender Bill'. You should call it that too. In fact, that's what we'll all be calling it.'

Bunter considered. 'I like that. The Surrender Bill. Yes, I like it a lot. What is it?'

Kaminsky sighed. 'It'll force you to ask for an extension to leaving the EU if you don't get a deal before the 19th of October.'

'But I'm not going to agree to an extension. I thought we were clear on that.'

'If they get this through then you'll have to.'

'Who's in charge around here?' said Bunter, adopting a sulk. 'I won't do it.'

There was a tap at the door, and Mandy entered. 'You've been summoned, Prime-Minister.

Bunter swung his legs from the desk and straightened up with a worried look. 'Is it about the parking tickets? Because that wasn't me. I mean I wasn't driving. What's a poor chap to do if he has a puncture and his gasket explodes, or snaps, or whatever gaskets do?'

'It's not about parking tickets, Prime-Minister. It's Tufton Street. They want to see you.'

Kaminsky stood up at once. 'Let's go. We can't keep them waiting.'

'But it's wine time Friday. I need to chivvy up the troops,' complained Bunter.

'Not today.'

❖

Bunter and Kaminsky located Tempus-Fugitson seated in a vast oak panelled office in Tufton Street with his hands behind his head, humming Land of Hope and Glory to himself with a far away smile. A life-sized portrait of Margaret Thatcher dressed as Boadicea glowered at them from one wall. Everything in the room seemed to be tinted with shades of grey, including Tempus-Fugitson, who stirred as they entered. When he stood up to greet them he was tall and sharp limbed blessed with an improbable number of angles.

'Hullo Bunter, old man. Do take a seat.' He glared at Kaminsky. 'You too, uhm..?'

'Gregory.'

'Of course. Mr Gregory. Please be seated.'

Kaminsky rolled his eyes and sat down in a low leather couch.

'You can't just summon me, you know, old boy,' complained Bunter, 'not now I'm Prime Minister and everything.'

'I'm the Chairman of the ERG,' said Tempus-Fugitson, as if that should be answer enough for anyone.

Bunter tried out two chairs before finding one that was comfortable, prodding the grey upholstery with distaste. 'What exactly is the ERG?'

Tempus-Fugitson looked horrified. 'Has nobody explained it to you?'

'I know you helped Kaminsky here with our Leave campaign.'

Tempus-Fugitson looked at Kaminsky. 'I thought you were Mr Gregory?'

'Gregory Kaminsky. I was blessed with two names. It can be confusing.'

'Aren't you Russian?'

'I'm a Yorkshireman,' replied Kaminsky.

Tempus-Fugitson nodded. 'I see. We've spoken on the telephone I believe?'

'Many times. Can we get on with this before Hell freezes over?'

'You were explaining about the ERG?' said Bunter.

'The European Research Group,' replied Tempus-Fugitson.

'And what do you research?'

'Never mind that now. Everyone who's anyone is a member. You might even be a member yourself, but the membership records are a closely guarded secret, so I can't say.'

Bunter turned to Kaminsky. 'Am I a member of the ERG?'

'I doubt it,' said Kaminsky. 'There's a subscription to pay.'

'Tax deductible,' added Tempus-Fugitson with warmth. 'Anyway, that aside, the ERG is delighted to support you as our new Prime-Minister. Now we want to help you with your task of getting Brexit over the line.'

'Get Brexit Done,' said Bunter, repeating the mantra that had got him into office. He gave Tempus-Fugitson a tentative thumbs up.

'Of course. And as Secretary for the Nineteenth Century, I feel I will amply contribute to the strategy of government. But the ERG has some concerns about sustainability.'

'I'm working flat out on a green agenda,' said Bunter at once.

'No, no. Not that kind of sustainability. The ERG is more concerned with the sustainable nature of your government. With your modest majority. And with the Surrender Bill that's due to be debated in Parliament.'

Bunter pushed back his jacket and thrust his hands into his pockets. 'I don't think we need to worry too much about the Surrender Bill,' he said.

'Why on earth not?' said Tempus-Fugitson.

'Well—because I have a plan,' said Bunter, bursting with pride.

'What kind of plan?' interjected Kaminsky with suspicion. 'Have you thought it through?'

'Do tell,' said Tempus-Fugitson, pursing his lips.

'Well, erm… it seems to me that if we're all so worried about what Parliament will do, then why don't I just shut it down? Stop it debating the Surrender Bill?' said Bunter.

Tempus-Fugitson clasped his hands together in a monochrome ecstasy. 'Would you, Prime Minister? Can you even do that?'

'Aren't I the Prime-Minister? I can do anything I like, can't I?' he addressed his question to Kaminsky, who was lost in thought, holding the room in suspense while he considered the question. Finally he raised a finger in the air to command attention to his final judgement.

'Constitutionally,' he said 'you couldn't do it yourself. You'd have to advise the Queen to do it.'

'I mean what's the point of it?' Bunter grumbled on, 'The big decisions are made by the big people—people like me. And I will lead a government that will always get the big decisions right, you see if I don't'

'If you can get the Queen to prorogue Parliament, then this bill will never see the light of day,' said Kaminsky.

'Then that's what I'll do,' said Bunter emphatically.

'Callooh! Callay,' said Tempus-Fugitson, fluttering his bony hands in delight. 'Tea anyone?'

❖

In the plush Tufton Street lobby Bunter read the names on the board. It reminded him of the First XI leader board at Greyfriars, in which he had never featured. Of course, he could have if he'd wanted to. He had always been athletic.

'Thatcher Institute of Trade Strategy. TITS,' mused Bunter. 'Who thought of that. Was it Del Boy Trotter?' he ventured with a guffaw.

'They're very supportive of you,' said Kaminsky in a prickly tone.

'Our Home – Britain,' continued Bunter. 'Where've I heard something similar to that?'

'You're a member of that one yourself, Billy.' said Kaminsky.

'Good Grief, am I really? What about the IEF— Institute of Economic Folly?'

'They're very influential. They were the architects of your economic policy.'

'Why have I never heard of them?'

'You never asked about them before.'

'Well, I think I should jolly well know who they are, if they're that important.'

Kaminsky seemed to snigger. 'This is the centre of government. You're just a figurehead really. I thought you understood that?'

'But aren't I the Prime Minister?'

'Of course, Billy. Shall we go?' said Kaminsky, rubbing a hand over the stubble of his shaved pate.

The big Georgian doors swung open and a brick built man in a tightly fitting suit shouldered his way inside. 'Zdravstvooitye!' he greeted Kaminsky as he swept past with a curt gesture.

'Privet!' returned Kaminsky, looking uncomfortable.

'What did he just say, old boy?'

'I think he just sneezed.'

'Sounded like Russian.'

'Why would he speak to me in Russian?'

'Hmm…' said Bunter, looking uncertain, like somebody holding four aces who just lost a hand of poker to a royal flush. 'What's that one? Is that one of ours too?' said Bunter, pointing up at the board. 'Russia Britain Friendship Group.'

'You better ask your fiancé about that one. Come on,' and Kaminsky put a hand on Bunter's back and led him firmly to the doors.

'But what do all these people do, old man?' protested Bunter as he was steered into the street.

'Somebody has to run the country,' said Kaminsky.

❖

Entering Number 10, Bunter lifted an empty bottle of Chateau Rothschild from a plant pot. Wine-time Friday. Kaminsky had cried off as usual citing a late liaison with his laptop.

'Bunter's here!' roared Todd over his shoulder as he emerged from one of the offices brandishing a bottle of Champagne. 'Behave yourselves. Hullo, old man.'

'It is my home, after all,' said Bunter. 'Is there any tuck?'

'All laid out inside, Bunter. Betty's been to Fortnum's. And you'll never believe who's here,' he confided, putting a friendly arm around Bunter's shoulders. 'The Home Secretary herself. Although I don't imagine she's drinking alcohol.'

Bunter hauled his dishevelled presence into the office where Abba was playing in the background and a couple was carousing beside the photocopier. Rajmar Pandit was glowering at him in the middle of the room with her arms folded. She was dressed in a black uniform with a utility belt and 'Home Secretary' embroidered loudly on the breast pocket. Her face was darker than usual and streaked with something that looked like pond algae.

'There you are,' she snapped.

'Good heavens. What are you wearing?' said Bunter.

'I'm on manoeuvres tonight with the Met police. Arresting criminals. What are you doing?' she said in an accusing tone.

Bunter adopted a haughty air. 'I've just been to see the ERG.'

Pandit seemed pacified for the moment. 'Did you know your staff are all drunk?'

'Of course I did, dear lady. It's Wine Time Friday – a Number 10 tradition.'

'Since when?'

'Since I introduced it. We need to motivate the people that do the work around here. All for one and ah… and all for me,' he said, plucking a drooping ham roll from a platter on a desk. Tomato pips drizzled down his chin as he tucked in. 'Was there something?'

'We need to talk about Ireland.'

'Don't we have a Northern Ireland Secretary for that, old girl?'

'I'm not your old girl,' she returned with a stony face.

'That's not what I said. Or rather not what I meant. I meant to say…'

'Never mind. Can we talk?'

'Now? It's Wine Time Friday don't you know?'

'The Brexit negotiators have suggested border checks should take place between Great Britain and Northern Ireland, rather than at the Irish border,' said Pandit. 'they're at a stand-off.'

'Well they can't. I mean they won't. I think I've made that perfectly clear. Over my dead body. Who did I appoint Attorney

General? I really don't remember.'

'Lord Mauleverer. He's over there…' she pointed with distaste at a gaunt, spare man in a tweed suit and a party hat with streamers, who was drooling over a much shorter female intern over the other side of the room.

'Mauly, old boy,' called Bunter. 'Mauly!'

Mauly broke off his seduction and sauntered over. He had a languid air that sometimes lapsed into sleepiness. He was wielding a goblet of red wine. 'Can I help, old man?'

Abba's 'Knowing Me Knowing You,' was rasping from poor quality speakers.

'The Home Secretary seems to think we have a legal issue with the Northern Ireland border post Brexit,' said Bunter, raising his voice.

'Yes, I'd heard about that. A tricky one if you ask me.'

'But I am asking you, Mauly, old bean.'

'Indeed,' said Lord Mauleverer with half closed eyes. 'Give me a moment,' and he seemed to contemplate the ceiling for several moments. Somebody burst a balloon. Raucous laughter ensued. 'Got it!' he said, finally.

'Already?' said Bunter, impressed.

'Well, I've thought of something we can propose instead.'

'So what is it?' pressed Pandit.

Lord Mauleveverer ignored Pandit and addressed Bunter. 'You remember the 1773 Inclosure Act?

'Er, vaguely old chap,' Bunter lied.

'It was very successful in greatly reducing the number of landowners in this country and tidying up large untidy areas of Common Land. What's more it's never been repealed,' said Mauleverer, shaking his head in apparent wonderment. 'So we simply apply it to both Northern and Southern Ireland, and make both countries the property of one landowner. The border ceases to exist, and with it so do any Brexit issues.'

'Isn't Ireland a separate country? Wouldn't that put a fly in the ointment?' said Bunter.

'Just a technical issue - we simply argue that the 1773 Act predates and therefore takes priority over the 1921 Independence Act.'

Bunter looked concerned and confused. 'Which landowner did you have in mind, old man?'

Lord Mauleverer thought for a moment. And his eyelids drooped. 'It would of course be an enormous responsibility, but one that I would be willing to take on for the sake of the sovereignty of our country and the greater good,' he replied, with a glow of munificence.

'So you're proposing we make you the owner of Ireland, Mauly?'

'What a splendid idea, Bunter. No wonder they made you Prime

Minister,' he said, patting Bunter on the arm. 'Of course, the Mauleverers have been substantial landowners for generations, so you've chosen a family that possesses exactly the right pedigree.'

'I've never heard such a stupid idea in my life,' said Pandit with a fierce look. 'I must go,' she said, consulting a large chronometer with an array of dials and buttons. 'I have doors to break down.'

Chapter Six

As BUNTER AND Singh passed through the police cordon outside Westminster they came across a battered, greasy man with a ragged beard sitting on the pavement wrapped in a blanket. A cardboard sign was propped in his lap. 'Brexit Casualty. Please feed.'

Bunter stopped in his tracks and reached inside his jacket, withdrawing a wallet than was plumper than he himself. He thumbed through a wad of notes and brandished a fifty-pound note, which he flapped at the man.

'I must give you something to keep yourself warm old fellow,' said Bunter in a compassionate voice. He rolled up the banknote, then took a match and set light to it, stooping to hand the flaming beacon to the beggar. 'This will soon get you warm,' he said with a wide grin.

The man desperately tried to extinguish the flames and salvage the money, but it had already turned to ash. He looked at Bunter without malice, shaking his head in disbelief.

'Wanker,' muttered the man in a hoarse voice.

Singh laughed. 'You really do put the 'large' into 'largesse' Bunter,' he said. 'Your humourfulness knows no bounds.'

Bunter looked pleased with himself. Then he said with vague remorse: 'I say, you don't think he was offended, do you?'

Singh looked back. A police officer was standing over the beggar as he packed away his meagre possessions. 'It was only fifty pounds. I think he would have seen the joke.'

A man in a blue top hat emblazoned with gold stars was shouting something through a megaphone as Bunter was hustled into the back of a Range Rover. Singh leapt in the other side.

'What about services, Prime Minister?' shouted the man in the hat. 'Is that part of your oven-ready deal, Prime Minister?' Bunter waved at him and smiled.

'What about services?' Bunter said in aside to Singh, settling into his seat. 'Is that part of our oven-ready deal?'

'I've been Chancellor for two days, Prime Minister. My unpreparedfulness for office is most legendary.'

Bunter considered. 'Are services important?'

'The man in the hat thinks ever so much so.'

As if to emphasise their importance the megaphone was pushed close to the window of the car and the man yelled: 'Services are 80% of the British economy and they're excluded from your deal, aren't they, Prime Minister! Admit it!'

'Is he right? The man in the hat? We, we must bake services into our deal,' said Bunter as the car whisked them away. When he looked through the rear window, he couldn't hear the man in the hat yelling at him any more, but he was standing in the middle of the road pointing his megaphone at the departing Range Rover and raising a fist.

'Into the oven ready one?'

'That's the one. Exactly, old chap.'

'Is it not one of half-bakedfulness already?'

'Just preparing the filling. Kneading the dough.' Bunter ruminated. 'Look at this...' Between them on the back seat was a hamper. Bunter lifted the lid and peeked inside. 'I had them prepare something for the journey.' He extracted a peach and bit into it, the warm juice dripping down his cheeks. 'Love peaches.'

'If you are needing the dough, perhaps you should not have come into politics?'

'You know what I meant. Not that kind of dough. Not that kind of kneading. Not that I don't need the dough, of course.'

'We're not going far, are we?'

'Oxfordshire. Always time for a snack, though,' he took another bite. 'Who was that man?'

'He's here a lot.'

'Rum chap.'

'Where are we going Prime Minister?'

'A photo op. Nothing to worry about.'

Singh looked at him with suspicion. 'Please to not tell me not to worry.'

Bunter laughed. 'We're going to DIG.'

'To dig?' repeated Singh with alarm. 'Are we to bury some person?'

Bunter laughed. 'Not dig. D.I.G. - It's one of our donors, an old chum. Lord Dovecote od Dovecote International Group. Here, have a pork pie...'

Singh pushed it away with revulsion. 'I don't...'

'Ah, no. Of course you don't.' Bunter stuffed it instead into his own mouth and the crumbs cascaded down his jacket. 'DIG makes diggers,' he mumbled thorough the remains of the pie.

'Diggers?'

Bunter swallowed, drawing a greasy hand over his mouth. 'Diggers, yes. You know - excavators. That sort of nonsense. Big exporter. Of diggers.'

'And why are we going there?'

'Oh, some Brexit stunt that Gregory dreamed up. Snappy will be there.'

'Snappy?'

'Don't you know anything, Inky? Snappy the photographer.' He waved out of the back window and a BMW flashed its lights. 'You know Snappy.'

Singh made a sour face. 'My pleasurefulness is replete,' he said.

'S'pose you don't want a glass of champagne?' said Bunter, extracting a bottle from a fridge between the seats.

'Might you have any Whiskey?'

'I thought you people didn't..? Never mind, old bean.' And Bunter produced a hip flask from his pocket. 'Here we are. Emergency rations.' Singh accepted it and took a long draught. Bunter leaned forward.

'How long to DIG?'

The driver was a thick waisted man with a stern demeanour. 'An hour. Maximum.'

Bunter thought for a moment. 'Are you Russian?'

'I'm from Peterborough,' he replied with thick Slavic vowels.

'Why is there so much traffic today?'

'They queue. Always they queue these days.'

'Queuing for what?'

'For tunnel of course.'

'There's a blockage in the Blackwell tunnel?'

'No. For Channel tunnel.'

'From here?

The driver shrugged his wide shoulders. 'Paperwork. What to do?'

Bunter and Singh paced side by side across a vast warehouse where they were greeted by a corpuscular man in a florid tie with alarming eyebrows. There was shuffling and muttering and a flutter of female laughter from beyond a partition that sectioned the warehouse in two. In front of the partition stood a gleaming white excavator with a twin cab. A union jack was draped over the bonnet, and emblazoned in blue and white on the shovel in letters four feet high were the words: 'GET BREXIT DONE'.

Bunter let out a wheezy laugh that was almost a cough and exclaimed: 'Digger, old fellow!'

The two men embraced, bumping bulbous tummies.

'Bunter, you old scoundrel!'

'Still digging for victory?'

'Still robbing the nation?'

Bunter looked hurt. 'I'm not.. It's not..' He gestured towards Singh. 'This is Inky. Actually, Singh. He's the Nabob of Bhanipur, y'know. Latterly Chancellor of the Exchequer. Everyone calls him Inky.'

'Not everyone,' interjected Singh, who looked unaccountably miserable.

Dovecote was mystified. 'The Nabob of what?'

'The importfulness of this title is lacking, Lord Dovecote.'

Dovecote extended his hand. 'Any friend of Bunter's is a friend of mine.'

'I am supremely overjoyed to make your acquaintance, sir.'

Dovecote looked at Bunter. 'Does he always speak like this?'

Bunter shrugged. 'He's a Greyfriars Old Boy.'

'That explains everything. Now, let's get cracking.' Ignoring Singh, Dovecote manoeuvred Bunter towards the excavator. 'Over there, the other side of that partition, we've assorted members of the press, plus your man Snappy. Usual suspects. Mail, Express, Telegraph. Somebody from Sky News. We've enlisted a few hundred DIG workers to make up the numbers, so it's quite a little crowd.'

'What do I need to do?'

'You and the Nabob chappie climb up into the cab, side by side.'

With unexpected agility, Dovecote halted himself up, tugged open the driver's door and leapt into the cab. 'Drives just like a car.' He pointed at the pedals at his feet. 'Clutch, brake accelerator. Ignition here. Just drive it straight into that wall and then stop after a few feet.'

'Into the wall?'

'It's a fake wall. The other side it says 'GRIDLOCK.' See? You're breaking through the gridlock.'

'This.,' he pulled a lever and the bucket raised. 'Raises and lowers the bucket. You don't need to touch it. In fact,' he raised a cautionary finger, 'don't touch it.'

Bunter looked doubtful. 'This is no more than a promotional video for DIG isn't it?'

'Nonsense. It's an election photo op. It was Gregory's idea entirely.'

Bunter wagged a plump finger at him. 'You put it into his head, didn't you, old bean?' He winked at Singh, 'Known him for years. Always the hustler.'

'Always the grifter,' returned Dovecote, and he jumped down and helped Bunter climb up. 'Get in the other side, would you, Nabob?'

'It's Ramset Jam Singh, actually,' mumbled Singh, walking around the cab and delicately climbing into the cab.

'So I bash though the bricks, and then..?' Asked Bunter.

'Then you make a bit of a speech, and that's it.'

'I'm ravenous.'

'There's a buffet and champers.'

'Excellent.' Bunter rubbed his hands at the prospect of food and alcohol. 'Well here we jolly well go.'

'And Bunter..?'

'Yes, Digger?'

'Say something nice about DIG.'

'Don't I always, old chap? The cheques are still rolling in, aren't they?'

As Bunter saw it, white plastic bricks flailing and falling and crashing past the cab window, it was a great success and he adopted a fixed and manic grin throughout that unnerved Singh and had him holding on tightly. That's how Singh spotted the girl as she disappeared under the Brexit shovel.

'You've hit somebody Bunter!' He yelled.

'Nobody important.' The digger had stopped and the engine was burbling. Bunter was making thumbs-up gestures through the window and raising and lowering the shovel, exactly as he had been told not to do. People were milling about the offside of the excavator.

'Everyone's important!' yelled Singh, scrabbling to get out of the cab. Bunter stepped down from the cab. Everyone was looking at a small pool of people gathered around a prostrate form. The prostrate form, Bunter noted, wore mesh stockings. He lumbered over, adopting the hangdog expression that won him votes. 'I'm so sorry,' he said.

The girl sat up. She was wearing a short leather jacket and had lion-like shoulder-length hair. She was half-dazed, half-angry, and fumbled for a Nikon camera hanging from her shoulder.

'You - you're Billy Bunter!' she said.

'I'm so terribly, terribly sorry,' said Bunter in the most sympathetic voice he could muster.

Dovecote appeared at his side, looking smug. 'I told you not to pull the lever, Bunter.'

'I don't think I can walk,' said the girl.

'Please don't sue,' begged Bunter. 'It wasn't even me that was driving. It was him. Inky. I mean Singh.'

Singh was horrified. 'I am… am full of horrorfulness at this accusation.'

'There, you see?' said Bunter, offering his hand. 'Barely speaks English. Shouldn't have allowed him behind the wheel. Awfully sorry. I'm the Prime Minister, y'know.'

'I know who you are,' said the girl, struggling to her feet and revealing herself to be a full-sized, woman-sized swan and not a girl, pretty in a tomboyish way.

'Please don't sue,' repeated Bunter.

'It was an accident,' said Dovecote. Two security guards had appeared from nowhere. The crowd was becoming restless. 'Take her somewhere to recover,' he said, and she was whisked away, struggling.

'No.. No,' said the woman. 'I wanted to... I wanted to ask you about the Russia Report. I'm a journalist, you see…"

But Bunter heard nothing more as he turned to the crowd and gave them a vigorous thumbs up with both hands. He yelled 'Get Brexit Done.' And there was a ripple of applause. He repeated his mantra and this time the applause was louder.

'I won't forget this,' muttered Singh as they both headed towards the improvised stage.

'I didn't.. I wouldn't have.. Lever was completely stuck. I thought you must have nudged me, old chap.'

'Nudged you? Of course.'

❖

'Get Brexit Done,' shouted Bunter from the podium. Singh stood beside him and tried to grin.

There was applause, but of course most of the audience had been coached. Photographers crouched and stalked and twisted lens barrels. Flashlights blinked.

'Thank you very much. It's wonderful to be back here in Kent at DIG.'

A ripple of laughter. Somebody shouted Oxford but nobody really cared.

'And DIG - one of the most amazing companies. Simply amazing. As we speak there are DIG diggers digging around the world. Around the world. And that's not easy to say, I can jolly well tell you.'

More laughter. Bunter, warming to his task.

'In every country in the world there are DIG excavators and back loaders - whatever they are. Clearing stuff. Mending stuff. Building stuff. And soon I'll be asking all of you. All of you here today and around the, around the country, to help elect a government to get clearing and mending and building. Because that,' gesturing frantically, 'that is what this country excels at,' and he thumped the lectern for emphasis. 'And, and what DIG excels at, of course, with their wonderful products, one of which I've demonstrated here for you today.

'Soon this country will be able to decide between going forward. Punching through the, errm, deadlock. The gridlock. And further delay and decay under a Beaver government - which will mean, which will mean more taxes and more rules and less nice stuff generally.' He held up a hand and there was applause. 'I say this:' he said, with as much emphasis as he could muster, 'we are going to beat that beaver. We are not going to let the beaver dam up our wages and our economy. And most of all, we are going to Get Brexit Done and get our sovereignty and our, and our control back. That's what we're going to do.' He pursed his lips and looked at the sky in the way that he'd seen Churchill do. Or Hitler. Somebody with history at his feet.

There was a tumult of applause. People were cheering. Bunter lifted an emperor-like hand and nodded. Nodded his approval. Then it was time for questions.

A small woman with a squeaky voice: 'When will we leave the EU?'

'As I've pledged. As I've said,' and he engaged her, speaking to her with a level gaze. 'It will be on 31st October. No ifs no buts.'

A resounding cheer went up.

'And,' he continued, 'or if not, then it will be very soon afterwards. Very soon.'

He gestured to accept another question. A big man whose nostrils seemed to have had all of the benefit of his hair growth had put up his hand. 'Will I still be able to buy things on Amazon?' He asked.

'Many people have asked this. Ordinary people just like you. And you have my word that Brexit will not affect your purchases of books, or, or CDs, or, or things that you may want to order from Amazon. Or anything else,' he finished with a flourish.

A man with a long lens camera had pushed to the front. He put his hand up and Bunter tried to ignore him, but he shouted his question.

'When will you publish the Russia Report?'

Bunter floundered for an instant and then adopted his most serious expression. 'It's, well as you know it's not up to me.'

'Did the Russians influence the referendum?'

'I want to … well as I'm sure you can understand,' he planted his hands on either side of the lectern, 'the public doesn't want to know about mythical Russian money. They want to know about our sovereignty as an independent nation. About controlling immigration. Bringing back control to our proud nation. And don't forget, we need to Beware the Beaver. That's the real threat. And of course, let's Get Brexit Done.'

The questioner's protestations were drowned in more applause, and Bunter left the stage with more thumbs-up gestures and cheery waves. Singh followed him without a word, and wondered why he had come at all. There were shouts of 'Prime Minister' but Bunter know better than to pay attention as he hurried away.

Chapter Seven

BUNTER PASSED THROUGH the Members' Lobby on his way to the Chamber for his very first PMQs. MPs reclined or slumbered on sofas or in armchairs waiting for the division bell that would call them to vote. Sleeping was a cross party activity. Some slumbered louder than others, and the occasional snort echoed off the vaulted roof. Bunter's stomach was unsettled. He thought he needed another breakfast.

'A word, Prime Minister!' Came an ominous call. Bunter turned to see Quelch striding towards him.

'Not now, sir. I mean, Lord. Your Lordship. I'm late.'

Quelch stopped and regarded him with a fearsome frown. 'Late? You're always late, Bunter. Quite soon you'll be late for good and your legacy will be nothing but tardiness.'

'I really don't have time,' said Bunter, flapping a palm at him. 'Why don't you have your secretary call my secretary and we'll put a date in the diary.'

'I need an undertaking from you, Bunter. I need to know when you're going to publish our report.'

Bunter was walking away, but Quelch was not giving up.

'Which report is that, old chap?'

'You know very well which report, Prime Minister.'

'It's not up to me. And if it was then I haven't read it. It's not ready. It hasn't been signed off.' He consulted his watch with a flourish. 'Must go, sir. I mean Quelch. Lord Quelch,' and Bunter ducked his head and strode away as fast as his bulk would allow, leaving Quelch with his hands on his hips, shaking his head.

Brian Beaver raised himself up on his toes at the despatch box. He was a slight and haggard man who aspired to be taller and less haggard, and his suit shone at the elbows. His grey beard was untrimmed. Still, he managed to view Bunter with disdain over his spectacles as the Speaker called the House to order and summoned him in a throaty monotonous tone:

'Leader of the Opposition!'

'Thank you, Mr Speaker. Firstly I would like to congratulate the Prime Minister on his appointment to the highest office.' A few disjointed 'Hear, hears' rose from the Conservative benches.

'Yesterday, Mr Speaker it was revealed that the Prime Minister's negotiating strategy with the EU is to run down the clock, and that the Attorney General told him that his belief that the EU would drop the backstop was a complete fantasy. Are these reports accurate, or can the Prime Minister provide the detail of his proposals to the EU?'

Beaver sat down after a rumble of support from the opposition benches.

Bunter rose to his feet and beamed all around the House. He hitched up his trousers, and touched the knot of his spotted bow tie then slapped a red folder on the despatch box. 'I'll tell you what. I'll tell you what our negotiating strategy is, Mr Speaker, it's to get a deal by the summit on 17th October and to take this country out of the EU on October 31st- to get Brexit Done! And what the Right Honourable gentleman's surrender bill will do is to, is to wreck any chance of the talks. Dither and delay is his strategy. 'What do we want: dither and delay. When do we want it? We don't know!' That's his, that's his policy. Now can he confirm that he will allow the people to decide in a General Election on October 15th? Or is he frit?'

Beaver took to the despatch box and cleared his throat. 'My first question to the new Prime Minister and no answer. I asked what proposals have been put to the EU? We've asked him many times, but he seems incapable of answering. The Prime Minister has said he's making progress, but the EU negotiator says no proposals have been received. Will he publish those proposals?'

'This government is going to get a deal with the EU,' bellowed Bunter in response. 'No ifs, no buts. They'll drop the backstop. They'll concede in every way. But we're not going to publish proposals because we don't negotiate in public. The only thing standing in our way is the surrender bill which will jolly well undermine our negotiating position.' Bunter was stabbing at the opposition leader with a forefinger. 'We delayed in March, we delayed in April, and now he wants to delay again for no purpose whatever. Dither and delay. All very silly. But here's the, here's the thing. We're going to spend a billion quid on police officers but he wants to spend a billion quid a month net to keep us in the EU. And I will never allow that.' Bunter snapped shut his folder and took to his seat amid shouts and jeers and flapping order papers. He suppressed a smirk. Things were going quite well, he thought.

The Beaver wasn't done with him. 'Mr Speaker - there are no negotiations to undermine. It's all a fiction. He's running down the clock. And when will he publish the Yellowhammer report showing the consequences of No Deal?'

'I'll tell you this. Negotiations are far advanced. A deal is close. But I know how much the Right Honourable Member worries about trade deals with the US - which are also far advanced - and chlorinated chicken. But there's only chlorinated chicken in the House and he's sitting on the opposition front bench! So can he confirm that he will let the people decide on the progress of negotiations, by agreeing to a General Election on October 15th?"

A surge of mumbled support arose as Bunter sat down again. He nudged Singh to his left and then Wharton to his right. Both nodded and smiled their approval. Prime Minister's Questions proceeded with its usual theatre with nobody any the wiser about anything. Which is just how Bunter would have liked. He rounded up with a final commitment:

'What this country needs is for a government to take this country out of the EU on 31st October and that is what I'm going to jolly well deliver. You see if I don't,' he raised a victorious fist and then plumped down onto the bench. Beaver glared at him from the opposition bench.

'I think I let him off lightly,' muttered Bunter. 'Right, I'm off to the Tea Rooms if anyone wants to join me.' And Bunter stood up and left the house, waving a casual hand at the Speaker.

Chapter Eight

BUNTER WAS IN his favourite place, nestling in that muffled vicinity somewhere between sobriety and inebriation but closer to the latter. People were laughing at his jokes and he was standing in the middle of the room with a glass in his hand. The glass, he thought, was half empty or half full, depending on your perspective. He waggled the crystal tumbler and somebody stepped in to top it up.

'This is my favourite place,' he confided to a jaded, portly woman in a tweed suit. He belched and the woman tried not to flinch.

'You're welcome to Belfast any time, Prime Minister,' said the woman, whom he thought to be familiar. She grimaced, which Bunter recognised was her distinctive way of smiling.

The journalists eddied around him like supplicants before an Emperor, and he wondered what he was going to say next. Often he found himself ambushed by his own words.

'It's nonsense,' he announced with trademark suppressed humour, 'that any sane person should imagine that Tato crisps from Tadagree Castle might be afflicted with some spurious tariff arrangement as a result of leaving the EU.' A ripple of laughter. 'Absolute piffle,' he added into his whiskey glass. 'And I'll tell you this: Northern Ireland has got a great deal. The best deal. You keep free movement. You keep access to the single market...'

'Won't there be a border, Prime Minister?' said a journalist.

'Not on any account.'

'How are we going to take control of our borders if there are no borders?' pressed the journalist.

Bunter glanced around the room for assistance, but Kaminsky was nowhere to be seen. He was feeling like he hadn't quite thought the matter through. He wagged a finger at the journalist. 'Don't you worry, we've thought about that,' he said. 'We've left no stone unturned in finding a solution, and I've put my best people on it.' He looked around the room. 'In fact, he should be somewhere around here.'

'So let me get this straight,' pursued the journalist. He was wide browed and intense and wielded a Bic pen with a broken cap. The UK has won control of its borders, but they won't apply to Northern Ireland?'

'It's not as simple as that, erm, actually.'

A big man with a florid complexion stepped forward with a heavy unsteady gait and said something cogent but incomprehensible.

Bunter leaned towards him. 'Sorry old chap. Would you mind saying that again?'

'Will there be a border between NI and GB?' said the big man, lifting his chin.

'Of course not. I'm even changing the stickers we put on our cars to demonstrate the fact that we're one big United Kingdom.'

'Stickers on cars?' said somebody in euphoria or bemusement.

'Indeed,' said Bunter. I'm the first person to have thought of it.

'Thought of what?'

'What's the first thing you think about when you hear GB?'

'Great Britain?' hazarded a woman.

'Precisely. But not Great Britain & Northern Ireland. So I'm making it absolutely clear. We are one family. We're all going to have to get brand new UK stickers for our cars,' he said with triumph.

'Oh well done,' said somebody clapping.

'Yes, well done,' said another.

'So, I can reassure my workers that we will not be filling in any customs declarations for our products leaving Northern Ireland to go to GB?' persisted the big man.

Bunter looked confused and put his head on one side. 'Could you just say that again?'

The man repeated himself and Bunter drew himself up in full affront. 'You most certainly can. And you can tell them from me, directly from the Prime Minister himself, that if somebody asks them to do that, they can ring up the Prime Minister and I will direct them to throw that form in the bin.'

The man shrugged and reached out to clink his glass with Bunter's. 'Good enough for me,' he said, spilling Bunter's replenished whiskey. 'Sorry, Prime Minister.'

The woman in the tweed suit was back at Bunter's side. 'You do know the DUP will no longer support this government if there's any kind of border? I've heard leaked reports there may be border checks in both directions.'

He looked at the woman and had the creeping realisation that this was Siobhan Fraser, leader of the Democratic Unionist Party. 'Aren't we paying you?' he said.

She grimaced. 'It's a matter of principle. Once bitten, twice shy.'

Bunter again looked around for Kaminsky, who was nowhere to be seen.

'There'll be no border. Trust me on that.'

'I don't have much choice, do I?' she said from the corner of her mouth.

'But we are paying you, aren't we?'

'I think the less said about that, the better, don't you?'

An attractive girl in an unseasonal summer dress with hair that looked like a lion's mane waved a microphone at Bunter.

'Prime Minister, can you please tell my readers something about the Russia Report? When will it be released?'

Bunter floundered. 'There isn't one,' he affirmed with an instinct honed at Greyfriars. 'What report? I know nothing about any report.'

'You almost killed me with your bulldozer,' she said. She had a crooked smile and flashing green eyes, and she seemed to hunch beneath the weight of her camera equipment.

Bunter was aware of other journalists taking an interest, and some of the invited Irish politicians. Where was Kaminsky, damn him? His security contingent were restless, patting their jackets as though to reassure themselves. This girl was fragile and pleading and didn't pose a threat. Unless he did something stupid.

'I think I'm going to faint,' said Bunter.

'What's all this? Who are you? Where's your press card?' Kaminsky had appeared out of nowhere with his brusque manner and piercing look. Bunter recovered himself just in time, straightening up and trying to look severe.

'I just want to know about the Russia Report,' said the girl. 'We've been promised…'

'This isn't the time nor the place,' said Kaminsky, summoning two plain clothes officers. 'Can we get this lady out of here?'

'You assaulted me,' said the girl. 'I've got it all on film. With a digger.'

Kaminsky rolled his eyes as she was led away, her cameras swinging against her hip. He turned to Siobhan Fraser. 'Everything all right?' he nodded at Bunter. 'His Maj?'

'We'll take care of it,' and she nodded at two implausibly tall, wide men who began quietly relieving assembled journalists of their cameras' memory cards. Bunter looked on with some disquiet.

'What's going on?' he said.

'Nobody makes a fuss in these parts,' said Siobhan Foster. 'Especially with a name like his.'

Kaminsky put a hand on Bunter's shoulder. 'Time to go, Billy.'

Chapter Nine

'THE VIDEO OF your performance in Belfast has gone viral on Twitter,' said Kaminsky with what Bunter thought was smug satisfaction. You've gained 22,000 followers and 82,000 likes. Of course, Siobhan made sure all the silliness was edited out.'

'I don't have a Twitter account,' said Bunter, attempting to light a huge cigar.

'Of course you do. It's one of the most active on Twitter.'

'Is it?'

'I particularly liked this Tweet of yours. Witty and succinct.' He swivelled his laptop around for Bunter to see.

'*Beaver may want to dam up the Northern Ireland economy, but we refuse to allow a border in Northern Ireland, soft or hard, and I was pleased to confirm this yesterday in Belfast. We are one United Kingdom.*'

'I didn't write that.'

'It's the kind of thing you might have written.'

'What else have I been tweeting?'

'We've tried to capture your wit and tenacity.'

'Let me see, then.'

Kaminsky turned the laptop around. 'Not now, Billy. We've got work to do.'

'Couldn't you have found a picture with my bow tie for my profile?' he complained.

Kaminsky ignored this. 'We need to talk about government communications.'

Bunter breathed a swathe of foul-smelling smoke across the table. It folded and lingered over the chestnut veneer.

'What kind of communications?' said Bunter.

'Deniable ones. Give me your phone.'

Bunter spun the phone once and then slid it across the desk. 'What do you want with my phone?'

'Do you use WhatsApp?'

'I don't follow, old chap.'

'WhatsApp. It's a messaging app.'

'Sorry old boy, you've lost me. I read Classics not Technology. I've tried to bring myself up to date. Even hired some American bimbo to tutor me on the techie stuff when I was Mayor, but we found we had other interests in common.'

Kaminsky shot him a stern look. Most of Kaminsky's looks were stern. Others were just intense. 'Pay attention, Bunter. I've loaded it on your phone. It works just like regular text messages except that these are encrypted. Look…' Kaminsky showed him as he pressed a green icon on Bunter's phone. Bunter blinked and observed without much interest. 'You'll use this for all communications with anyone that you want to keep private.'

'Like Iggy?'

'Definitely Ignatov and his father. But also your Cabinet colleagues. And me, of course.'

'Things we don't want the public to find out about?'

'You can set these messages to disappear.'

'I wish I'd known about this when I was Mayor. But listen, if I delete them on my phone, are they also deleted on the recipient's phone?'

'No. they'll also need to delete them. But that's only a problem if they know who the recipients are.'

'Who's 'they'?'

'I'm just preparing you, Bunter, for an apocalypse that may never happen.'

'Show me again how I can make messages disappear.'

Mandy tapped on the door. When she stepped through Bunter couldn't help but notice that her skirt was shorter even than yesterday. 'Your call with President Putin, Prime minister begins in five minutes.'

'Oh lor,' said Bunter. 'I'd completely forgotten.'

Kaminsky became animated. 'Mustn't keep the boss waiting.' They both rose and Kaminsky almost led Bunter by his elbow across the room, where Bunter slotted himself behind his desk, flanked by two Union flags beneath a gilt-framed portrait of the Queen.

Bunter scowled up at Kaminsky who was lingering in front of the desk. 'This is a confidential meeting between two heads of state.'

'It's fine, Billy. I'll read MI5's transcripts later.' Kaminsky gave an ironic salute and left, while Bunter waited for the video call to begin, fumbling to perfect the knot in his bow tie.

At length Putin appeared on Bunter's computer screen seated at the foot of a long table, wearing a grimace that served as a smile. He wore a dark suit and a red tie and Bunter thought he looked more self-assured than any leader had a right to be. 'Good morning Mr Bunter,' said President Putin in flawless English, 'May I offer my belated personal congratulations on your accession?'

'Good morning, Mr, ah, President. So glad that you could spare the time from your busy schedule.'

Putin looked at a rock of a watch that gleamed on wrist. 'I can give you three minutes.'

'Thank you, sir. I mean Mr President. Well look, firstly I want to make our position clear on the Salisbury poisonings.'

'You've already done that,' said Putin with impatience.

'Have I? Have we?'

'Of course. You summoned our ambassador. We summoned yours. Etc, etc.' He flapped a dismissive hand. 'Let's put all this unpleasantness behind us and start as we mean to go on.'

'Urm, yes. Of course.'

'We have a glorious history, our two nations,' began Putin, 'as allies in a generational war against the acquisitive ambitions of the French. We were once united against a European empire led by Napoleon. In the end of course, my ancestor Alexander was forced to defeat the French alone…' he continued in a lengthy diatribe against Europe in general and France in particular.

'But surely you aren't a descendent of Tsar Alexander?' interrupted Bunter.

Putin smirked. 'How would you know that?' He folded his hands on the table, glancing again at his watch. 'In any event, we find ourselves once again allied against the imperial French, and this time I propose we face them together. Once you have shrugged off the chains of the EU, Russia and England can enjoy a renewed friendship and affluence. We can talk about trade deals, and even embargos against the perfidious French. Perhaps in time, England could even form part of our Commonwealth of Independent States?'

'Well of course, Great Britain welcomes any trade deals once we are outside the EU.'

'I think we can do better than that. Much better. For too long England has been in thrall of the United States and NATO. Now might be the time to lose those shackles and form a new alliance with a stronger partner.' Putin looked again at his watch. 'There will be time for these discussions, and I look forward to welcoming you to Moscow for talks. Now I must attend to matters of state. I've enjoyed our outline discussions on our new partnership and free trade deal. We will issue a press release.'

'Mr President... I wanted to ask about the Crimean bridge...' but the screen was already blank. Bunter had a sneaking suspicion that he was being manipulated.

Chapter Ten

IT SEEMED TO Bunter that the formal rooms of Balmoral were tainted with the smell of woodsmoke, dampness and dogs' piss. He had been led down draughty corridors with creaking boards by a creaky limbed man in a morning suit who had barely said a word. Bunter wondered if he even knew who he was. He was shown into a room that looked like a museum gallery, with mouldings and cornices and threadbare Afghan rugs. There was a fire crackling in the grate and a Dyson air purifier beside the fireplace, labouring to remove the odours. A gilt framed landscape depicted a scene that looked like the Bosporus. The Queen, dressed in a pale floral dress held out a tentative hand and he took it as firmly as he dared. He bowed.

'It's always cold in here,' said the Queen, wringing her hands.

'Your majesty,' said Bunter. He looked down to find a corgi

sniffing at his trouser leg. He nudged it with a toe. In photographs, the Queen always seemed to be smiling, but today she wore a distinct frown.

'In my experience as regent, Prime Ministers rarely seek an audience with us more than once: on appointment and on resignation. As I seem to recall you coming here to be appointed not long ago, then I assume it's for the latter.'

Bunter was at once abashed and disconcerted. 'Ah, no your majesty. Not really. Not at all.' He shuffled a foot to deter the continued interest of the corgi. 'I'm delighted to continue as your loyal servant…'

'Oh, stop it. We've had quite enough of that sycophantic nonsense. If it's not that, then it must be something else. What do you want? Can't you see one is busy?'

Bunter cast a glance around the room with its framed photographs on lace shrouded coffee tables and its spartan furnishings. It didn't look to be a hive of industry.

'I've come here today…'

'Yes, yes. We can rather see that, can't we? Do get to the point.'

'I'm sorry, your majesty,' he said, feeling out of breath.

'We already know why you're here,' said the queen, 'but you're supposed to tell us, and not keep one guessing.'

'Of course. I do apologise. But I'm not here to resign. I have a mandate. The people's mandate. What I'm seeking ma'am is your permission to prorogue parliament from the second week in September until the fourteenth of October.'

'You can't prorogue it.'

There was a lengthy pause, in which Bunter wriggled with discomfort. 'Why not?' he ventured at last.

'You can't prorogue it because it's not yours to prorogue. Only we can do that.'

'And may I ask, who is 'we'?'

'ME you buffoon. As regent one employs the royal 'we'. If you want to be 'King of the World' as I've heard that you do, then you'll need to brush up on your royal etiquette,' she gave a little chuckle. 'Anyway, why would you want to prorogue Parliament? It's only happened twice since Charles I did it in 1628. You'll be creating history.' The Queen sat down on a pale green velour couch and did not invite Bunter to do the same. 'The last time it happened was when that nice Mr Major requested it. And that, if we recall, was to avoid debate of some grubby shenanigans involving money. It all ended in tears, as we believe we told Mr Major it would at the time.'

'We're going to bring forward a new bold and ambitious domestic legislative agenda for the renewal of our country after Brexit,' said Bunter, repeating the wording that Kaminsky had outlined in a WhatsApp message only an hour before.

The Queen let out a lengthy sigh. 'Oh, that old thing. Haven't you got your Brexit thingy done yet? It really is quite tiresome.'

'Not quite yet, your majesty. But it will be done on 31st October,' said Bunter, 'No ifs, no buts,' he added without much conviction. He felt the urge to give the queen a thumbs up gesture to reinforce the message, but stopped himself just in time.

'Yes, I'm sure you think it will. We still don't understand why you believe there's a need to prorogue Parliament.'

'It's to prepare your majesty's speech for a new session of parliament. We need to get on with our plans to take the country forward.'

'But it's hardly orthodox,' said the Queen, gazing at the ceiling. 'And our speech is by tradition rather a slapdash affair. It shouldn't take long to write it. We wish sometimes one would include a few witticisms. It makes us appear such a dour monarch. Not to mention rather dim. We could write it ourselves.'

'It's just meant to set out your government's agenda, your majesty. And our agenda this time is stacked with groundbreaking…'

'Nothing to do with preventing debate of the Surrender Bill, then?' said the queen with sudden intensity.

Bunter's knees began to quiver. 'I'm sorry your majesty, I haven't the faintest idea…'

'At least that much is probably true,' she cut in. 'Don't think we don't know your game, Mr Bunter. Remember we've outlasted 15 of you lot, and we've no doubt there'll be more of you before we pass on.'

'Is that a yes, your majesty?' pursued Bunter in a timid voice.

The Queen suddenly looked very sad. 'We are only ceremonial these days,' she said, watching another corgi take an interest in Bunter's trouser leg. 'One has limited powers.'

'I'm sure that's not strictly true, your majesty.'

'Off with his head!' snapped the queen. With a wistful smile the Queen watched Bunter quivering before her. Moments later, nobody had rushed through the doors to carry out her command, and she heaved another long sigh. 'You see?' she said. 'In my grandmother's day you would have been dragged at once to the scaffold.'

'I'm sure you didn't mean…'

'Oh, get out, Mr Bunter. You can have your prorogation of parliament. Just don't expect us to pick up the pieces afterwards.

Bunter bowed low and backed away.

'And one other thing…'

'Anything, your majesty.'

'We would like some jokes in our speech. Keep it light-hearted. We've already had quite enough annos horribilis for any reign.

Chapter Eleven

'SO NOW WE have it?' said Kaminsky. 'We have the suspension of Parliament?'

'Like putty in my hands, she was,' yawned Bunter, munching on a doughnut, his bow tie unfastened and dangling from his collar.

'I'm so proud of you,' said Marianne, perched on the arm of the couch in their apartment at Number 10.

'It wasn't all plain-sailing of course,' said Bunter, keen not to minimise his achievement. 'But when I turned on the Bunter charm she couldn't resist. A game old bird, I thought.'

Marianne shoved him. 'Billy. Less of that.'

Bunter leaned over the coffee table and scribbled a few lines onto a foolscap pad, then thought hard. Kaminsky sat opposite, with his fingers steepled. The coffee table was loaded with snacks and bottles of wine. Bunter took a slurp at his glass and sighed in satisfaction.

'Now,' said Kaminsky, 'we need to turn to the rebels.' He scanned Bunter's bookcase with idle curiosity: Winston Churchill's 'History of the English Speaking People'; a copy of 'Our Island Story'; Bunter's very own bonkbuster, 'My Uncle's Harem'. 'It's the time to be strong Billy. That lot in the House betrayed you – it's their fault that you've had to resort to proroguing parliament and now they've got to go.'

'They betrayed you,' echoed Marianne.

'Eh? What? Go? Go where?' Bunter looked up from his writing.

'What are you doing, Billy?'

'Deadline from my publisher, old bean. I've already missed three.'

'But what are you writing?'

'A sequel.'

'My Billy's not just Prime Minister, he's a best selling author,' said Marianne with pride..

'A sequel? A sequel to what?'

'Our Island Story. It's most awfully exciting. I'm taking Henrietta Elizabeth Marshall's fabulous portrayal of the history of our proud nation and bringing it bang up to date. Up to the bit where we leave the EU, in fact.'

'Isn't it a children's book? Full of patriotic nonsense about empire?' said Kaminsky.

Bunter looked aggrieved. 'A children's book, you say? Certainly not, old man. This is weighty history. Like Tacitus.'

'You need to focus on the job in hand, Billy.'

'Well, yes,' conceded Bunter, 'But the day job barely pays for Marianne's dress maker. Need to keep the wolf from the door, old boy. I can't get Digger to pay for everything—even if he has been most awfully generous.'

'Matters of state, Billy. Matters of state matter more.'

'I didn't know it was a children's book. Are you certain, old chap?' said Bunter, perplexed.

'The rebels, Billy. Focus. We need to eject them from the Party. All 21 of them.'

Kaminsky made a dramatic cutting gesture.

'You mean withdraw the whip? From all of them?'

'Of course, we must! Do you think Ivan the Terrible could have conquered Kazan and Astrakhan if he hadn't tossed out the Boyars?'

'I hadn't cast myself as Ivan the Terrible. At least not that terrible.'

Kaminsky stands up, looking around the room for inspiration. He sees a bust of the Roman emperor, Nero, and places his hand on its head.

'What about Nero. Could he have crushed Boudicca and the Parthians if he hadn't set fire to Rome?'

'I know something about that. Nero features in "Our Island Story." Although as you know I'm more Ancient Greece than Ancient Rome.'

'The rebels, Billy,' said Kaminsky, making a fist.

'I say old chap - these are decent fellows you know. Some of them even went to Greyfriars.'

'Precisely! One of them might stand against you as leader of the party. Expunge them now, Billy and you'll be the new, unchallenged, Emperor of Britain! With a stonking majority at the next election.'

Marianne absent-mindedly reaches for the flowers in the vase and starts twirling them in her fingers. Bunter strokes his chin. 'Emperor you say. Interesting thought. Like Napoleon,' said Bunter, tucking a hand inside his jacket. 'He unified Europe into one successful trading block, created a single currency. France was a military superpower, and everyone got rich. Maybe if I was Emperor we could try something similar?'

Kaminsky looks alarmed. 'No! No! No! Wrong image completely! That's not want we want to achieve at all. Divide and rule. Make your enemies in Europe weak so you can look strong. Get Brexit Done—that's the single message. Am I not getting through to you?' He snatches up one of the volumes of Churchill's "History of the English speaking people". Be a man that changes history - like Churchill!'

Bunter looked thoughtful.

'Churchill eh? By George I think you've got it. He gave a thumbs up. 'Get Brexit Done. Righto.'

'Like Churchill! Fight them on the beaches. Don't buy cars and washing machines from them! I have to go now for a meeting with Wolf. But before I go, promise me that you will plan to expel the rebels from the party, now and forever!'

Bunter looked hesitant. 'Rum chap, that Wolf.'

'He's your biggest ally.'

'Wasn't he in the KGB when it was still called that?'

'Everyone was in the KGB in those days.

Bunter sighed. 'I expect so. Well, if you think it's for the best, old bean...'

'Now, you need to come up with a strategy. You can't just haul them all in one after another.'

Bunter thought for a moment. 'I rather thought I could send them a text.'

'A text?' repeated Kaminsky. 'Masterful.' He headed for the door.

'It's for the best, Billy, it really is. Don't weaken! See you at the cabinet meeting tomorrow.'

The door closed softly behind him and Marianne turns to Bunter.

'The Russians are our friends, Billy.'

Bunter reached for another doughnut. 'Yes, I've been meaning to ask you about that. About the Russia Britain Friendship Group. In Tufton Street. So, what's all that about?'

Marianne nestled beside him and took one of his hands. 'I'm doing it for you, Billy. You know, France and Russia were once allies? If Napoleon hadn't reneged on the deal they would have ruled Europe together. Alexander and Napoleon.'

'Didn't Alexander defeat Naploeon?'

'Yes, and we wouldn't want history to repeat itself, would we? That's why we need the Russia Britain Friendship Group to keep Putin close. That's why you need to be strong, like Alexander.'

'Alexander, you say? Well, if that's what you want Piglet. I'll throw the Christians to the lions first thing in the morning. After breakfast, of course. I'll need plenty of sustenance. Emperors do, you know. Maybe I should write a book about Alexander, what d'you think? I'll talk it over with my agent.'

The Cabinet room smelled of beeswax and stale cigars. Rain stippled the glass of the casement windows. There was an of end of term mood, with all the usual suspects playing up more than usual. Bunter presided at the end of the table with a broad smile on his face.

'I say, come on chaps,' he said. 'let's have some order about the place.'

'Do I take it, Prime Minister, that those of us around this table are the survivors of your purge?' said Tempus-Fugitson.

Bunter was contemplating a cream bun presented on Number 10 porcelain. 'I think that's a fair analysis, Tempus old fellow. Unless you got a text,' he said, nudging the bun with a forefinger as though to test his restraint.

'I received no such thing,' said Tempus-Fugitson with smug fortitude.

'Where is the Right Honourable Johnny Bull, Secretary for Levelling Up?' inquired Cherry with angel-face insouciance.

'Levelled, I'm afraid to say,' said Bunter.

There was a tap on the door and Mandy put her carefully coiffured head inside without waiting for an answer.

'Cabinet is in session,' said Bunter in a pompous voice.

'I'm sorry Prime Minister, but this can't wait.'

Bunter cast an apologetic glance at his assembled Cabinet. 'The travails of high office, I'm afraid.'

'It's your son,' said Mandy. 'He says it's very urgent.'

'Oh lor. Which one?'

'Damien.'

'I see—that one. He'll be asking for money, I expect. Missing postal order,' said Bunter, reminiscent of his days at Greyfriars waiting for an elusive postal order from his father that never arrived.

'How many sons have you got?' wondered Cherry.

Bunter paused to make a mental calculation. 'That depends…'

'Depends on what?'

'Do we still have postal orders?' mused Pendlesham, who as Trade Secretary felt that she ought to know.

'Damien…' Bunter addressed Mandy with caution, 'Is that the one who's still at University or the one who writes for that ghastly men's magazine? Tell him I'm in Afghanistan or something, inspecting the troops. Tell him I can't be reached today. Or ever.' He bit on a croissant which sent a cascade of flakes down his tie 'I might die, you know,' he added with a hurt expression.

'Lord Quelch is still on hold. It's been an hour. And several MPs about a text message?'

'Tell Quelch the same thing.' Bunter rolled his eyes at Kaminsky sitting at the side of the room with his legs crossed. 'The Russia Report.'

'It's in hand.'

'In whose hand?'

Kaminsky coughed into his hand and reached for a battered leather attaché case at his feet. 'I'm authorised to let you see a draft. I've been meaning to tell you.'

The members of the Cabinet, suddenly attentive, leaned forward in unison.

'Authorised? Authorised by whom? Why would I need authorisation?'

'We've been over this, Billy,' said Kaminsky, shuffling through some documents. 'Here it is,' and he stood and hefted a thick document onto the table.

Bunter fanned through the pages. 'Why are all the words blacked out?'

'Redacted.'

'But there's nothing left.'

Kaminsky said nothing, simply smiled faintly.

'Beaver won't wear this, old man.' said Bunter.

'Beaver won't last beyond the election.'

'Is this an agenda item?' said Cherry.

'It's important that we are united on the response to this, chaps, when it becomes public knowledge.' said Bunter, flapping the report. 'We must make sure there are no divisions.'

'Division!' bellowed Dutton, struggling to his feet and upsetting a glass of water whose contents cascaded over the edge of the table. 'Division!'

'Calm down, you old coot,' said Truscott.

'Eh? What?' said Dutton, his eyers darting around the room in suspicion.

'Sit,' said Bunter with an imperious gesture, and Dutton sat down in a pool of water.

'The kindest thing would be to have him put down,' said Pandit.

Dutton glared at her.

Kaminsky muttered something unflattering that may have included the words 'dementia,' and 'addled'.

'Where was I?' said Bunter.

'We were just finishing up,' provided Cherry.

'Yes, of course. I call this Cabinet meeting to a close.'

Chapter Twelve

'I SAY, IGGY is he safe?' said Bunter, shrinking from a large and languorous leopard that was baring its teeth at him.

'Billy!' snapped Ignatov.

Bunter started. 'Yes, old man?'

'I was talking to the leopard,' said Ignatov, tugging at a sturdy chain.

'You call him Billy?'

'She,' said Ignatov. The leopard yawned and settled on its haunches, eying Bunter with hungry eyes. 'It's not named after you.' Ignatov assured, leaning forward in the couch and patting the Leopard on its head. 'although I do have a small puppy that I call Bunter.' Ignatov grinned.

Bunter wriggled in his armchair and looked hurt. 'I don't know how I feel about that.' An improbably beautiful girl offered him a glass of whisky on a silver platter and took his empty glass away with an elegant, alabaster hand. Bunter thought she smelled of honeysuckle when she leaned down to him.

'Wonderful,' he said, trying to catch her eye.

'We shouldn't be seen together too much at the moment, Bunter. Not before the election.'

'It's in the bag, dear boy,' said Bunter with a dismissive gesture.

Ignatov frowned. 'We almost need Beaver to win a reprieve on Brexit.'

'What for? I promised the voters no ifs and no buts.'

'Politicians' promises are not the same as real promises. It'd rather suit your election campaign to whip up the racists and the rabble against the opposition. In their eyes, it'll be Beaver that defies your best intentions to get Brexit done and deliver the will of the people.'

'So, we don't want to Get Brexit Done any more?' said Bunter, perplexed.

'Of course we do—just not yet. We want to create a lot of noise about getting Brexit done, and then blame Beaver and the EU Commission for creating obstacles. That will be the tone of the leaders in all my papers.'

'I see,' said Bunter, not seeing.

'The priority for all of us is to get you re-elected with a fat majority and make you unassailable. Then you can pass any bill you like— including a no deal Brexit.'

'And do you think that's what the public wants?'

'They don't know what they want until you tell them.'

Bunter made a hesitant thumbs up.

Ignatov stroked his perfectly groomed beard. Everything about Ignatov was perfectly groomed, even down to his eyelashes. His suit looked like it cost more than Bunter's car and was certainly cleaner—the pockets were also not stuffed with unpaid parking tickets. 'From now until the election you need to be more visible, Bunter. Perform some of your clownish stunts. I'll make sure the paps are there to record them.'

'Stunts? said Bunter, offended.

'Start tomorrow,' said Ignatov with finality, rattling the leopard's lead. The leopard looked up and bared its teeth again at Bunter.

'I was thinking…' said Bunter.

'I meant to suggest that you don't do too much of that. Leave it to the adults.'

'Iggy, that's quite enough.'

'Sorry Bunter,' said Ignatov, laying a hand on Bunter's knee. 'You know I'm full of respect for what you've achieved.'

'Yes, well,' said Bunter, finishing his whisky. 'But I was wondering… just how long is the Crimean bridge?'

Ignatov looked puzzled. 'I believe it's about 19 kilometres. Why would you want to know?'

'And who built it?'

Ignatov shrugged. 'How would I know?'

'An engineering feat worthy of Balfour,' mused Bunter.

❖

'Where did you get that hat?' said Marianne with distaste the next morning, from her perch at the breakfast bar where she nudged muesli around a small puddle of oat milk in a bowl.

'Just part of the image, my dear' said Bunter, pouring a glass of orange juice. 'It's Iggy's idea to make me more attractive to the masses.'

'You're also wearing a track suit,' observed Marianne. 'You've never worn a track suit in all the years I've known you.'

'I'm going to exercise,' announced Bunter with pride.

'Don't you need a priest for that?' said Marianne.

'Exercise, not exorcise Piglet. You know full well. I'm going jogging.'

'Jogging.'

'Just a few rounds of some trees, I expect. Nothing too taxing. More of a photo op. Iggy's lined up some paps and so has Rupert.'

'Paps,' said Marianne. 'You used to hate the press. Even when you worked for The Spectacle.'

'Yes, but that was before they were on our side.'

There was a tap on the door of the kitchen.

'Yes?' barked Bunter.

A functionary that Bunter had not seen before opened the door. 'The police are here.'

'The police? Tell them I'm not here. Whatever it is I wasn't there at the time. In fact, tell them I'm in consultation with my lawyers.'

'It's your security detail Mr Bunter.'

Bunter frowned. 'Is that an East European accent?'

'I am immigrant from Stevenage.'

'I don't think people from Stevenage are usually seen as immigrants.'

'They are if they are coming originally from Kazan. In Russian Federation.'

'I see. Well, welcome.'

'Spasibo. Thank you.'

The two hulking Special Protection officers Bunter first encountered at the airport bustled into the room wearing identical tracksuits and expensive trainers.

'Ah. It's you,' said Bunter.

'At your service, Prime Minister,' said one, with irony.

Bunter absorbed their track suits and trainers. 'We're not going miles and miles.' The two officers looked at each other, then turned to leave. 'Where are you going?'

'We thought you just said we weren't going.'

'Oh goodness gracious. I meant we're not going FOR miles and miles. I didn't mean "We're not going, Miles and Miles." You know perfectly well what I meant. The comma was implicit,' said Bunter with an aggrieved look.

'No sir, we certainly didn't know what you meant,' said one Officer Miles with a suppressed smile. 'Implied commas wasn't on the curriculum at Hendon.'

'Well then you jolly well should.'

'What's the hold up?' said Bunter later, slumped in the back of an official Range Rover and feeling exhausted already. His trainers were hurting. Miles and Miles were in an identical Range Rover behind. Both cars and an accompanying police car were at a standstill on Whitehall.

'Same like last time. Brexit traffic,' said the driver over his shoulder.

In front of them was an articulated truck bearing French plates and a sign written trailer that read 'Le Grand Fromage.'

'It's all these bloody foreigners,' grumbled Bunter. This is the reason we need to get Brexit done.

'I despise foreigners,' said the driver with slurred syllables.

'But didn't you say you were Russian?'

'From Ryazan, yes. It's not the same as foreigner.'

'I suppose not,' said Bunter with a squirm. 'Can't you do something about the traffic?'

'We can use lights and sirens.'

'Please do.'

'Just like Moscow,' said the driver in delight, engaging the blue lights and nosing up to the truck which pulled onto the pavement almost knocking over a man in a blue top hat carrying a placard that read: 'Join this Traffic Queue for Brexit.'

'We need a Helipad in the Rose Garden at Number 10,' said Bunter.

'In Soviet times I flew helicopters in Afghanistan,' said the driver over his shoulder. 'Four AT-6 Spiral missiles would make short work of traffic queues, yes?'

'How long did you say you've you been in the UK exactly?' said Bunter with unease.

'More than 6 weeks,' said the driver. 'It is shithole,' he added in further clarification, swinging the wheel to avoid a black cab. Bunter found himself thrown against the door, reaching for the grab handle.

'So how did you end up here, working for us?'

The driver shrugged. 'I go where I am told.'

Bunter considered this. 'Have you ever been to Crimea?'

'I did some work there. It was tragedy,' he said, shaking his head.

'It most certainly was,' Bunter agreed.

'How dare Crimea try to invade Russia. It is good that Putin is strong leader, yes?'

'That's one way of looking at it.' They had picked up speed now. 'I think we can lose the sirens.'

'Sure boss,' said the driver with evident disappointment.

A thought occurred to Bunter. 'So, do you know anything about the Crimean Bridge? I was only talking to a chum of mine about it yesterday.'

'Kerch Bridge? I was involved in such project, yes.'

Bunter leaned forward with renewed interest. 'Do you know much about it?'

'Ask me anything.'

'How long is it?'

'Longest bridge in Europe,' he said with pride. '19 Kilometres.'

'What would that be in miles?'

'Shorter,' said the driver after a moment's thought.

'Never mind. I'll get somebody to work it out. And do you know who built it?'

'Of course. It was Putin.'

Bunter sighed. 'Yes, but he didn't build it personally, did he?'

The driver let out an alarming guffaw. 'Of course not. One of his companies made this bridge. Some oil and gas company.' He strained to turn his head and tapped the side of his nose. 'Of course, this not public knowledge.'

'You can trust me,' said Bunter, 'I'm the British Prime Minster.'

The driver seemed to find this immensely funny, and laughed until it brought on a coughing fit, which caused the Range Rover to career across the road. Bunter pushed himself back in his seat and tensed for a collision, but none came, and the driver assumed control again, slapping the steering wheel. 'Funny,' he said with suppressed humour.

'Do you have a problem, Big Dog One?' said an urgent voice over the radio.

'No, no. Just rabbit in road,' said the driver with a conspiratorial glance at Bunter.

'Did you say a rabbit, Big Dog One?'

'What do I know? I'm not fucking Richard Attenborough. Maybe was a hare.'

'Big Dog One?' queried Bunter after the radio lapsed into silence.

'It's you, yes? Big Dog. Big Dog One is call sign.'

'I like that,' said Bunter with a wistful feeling that he had finally turned his back on the obscurity of his years at Greyfriars. He'd never really had the recognition of a nickname before unless you counted 'That Fat Oaf'.

They were lying in wait at Regent's Park. Boxy, big shouldered, bearded men in fatigues, weighed down with canvass bags and back packs. They raised their equipment and sighted Bunter's car as it swept up to the kerb. The press pack was here, as promised.

Bunter levered himself from the rear of the Range Rover and gave the pack a jaunty wave. Miles and Miles joined him, and Bunter gave a brief display of on the spot running and stretching for a few breathless moments, before setting off into the park at a leisurely pace, followed by his security detail and the paparazzi. After 50 metres or so, Bunter glanced back to see two uniformed policemen intercept the photographers, just as he and the Mileses ducked out of view behind a coppice of trees that shielded from view a small café. A solitary pedestrian sucked on a polystyrene cup at a rusting, uneven iron table.

'You'll have to move, sir,' said one of the officers, flashing some ID.

The man looked bewildered. He had a folded copy of the Guardian beside him and wore a grubby anorak. 'What on earth for?' He glared at Bunter.

'It's the Prime Minister, sir.'

'I know who it is.'

'We're his security,' said the other Miles, 'and you're going to have to move along.'

Bunter stood a few paces away in the shadow of a broad bodied eucalyptus with cracked bark. A crumpled cigarette packet and a McDonalds carton lay in the lee of the tree. A pedestrian passed by and stared. Bunter looked up at the sky: it looked like rain again.

'Why should I?' the man was saying. 'What gives you the right?'

'I don't want to have to forcibly remove you, sir.'

The man looked at his cup. 'I've paid for this coffee.'

'You can take it with you.'

'I didn't vote for that fat oaf.' He stood up. 'and I'll not be voting for him next time.' He shook his newspaper at Bunter and shambled off down the path. Bunter took his seat.

'What have they got to eat here?' said Bunter.

The Mileses exchanged glances. 'Is that it, then?'

'Is that what, old man?'

'Is that as far as we're going to run?'

'I think I've pulled a hemlock or something,' said Bunter, rubbing his ankle. 'I think that's enough for one day. Would one of you mind stepping into the chair and getting a couple of bacon rolls and a latte? I've left my wallet at Number 10 and all this jogging has given me quite an appetite.' He pointed. 'We'll do a turn around that oak tree in 20 minutes or so and then rejoin the press on the way back to the car. And if they've got any muffins I'll have three. Get one for yourselves,' he added with generosity.

After Bunter had eaten four bacon sandwiches with extra HP sauce, three blueberry muffins, and two toasted cheese sandwiches, he signalled that he was ready to resume his exercise. A small huddle of dogwalkers and joggers had clustered not far away, and some were taking pictures with their phones.

'It can't do any harm,' said Bunter. 'They've got to learn I'm just like them. A man of the people, that's how I'd like to be known.' He beamed at his security detail. 'Now let's get going. Not too quickly as now I have this hemlock strain.'

The press was at the park gates. Some were kneeling and wielding long lenses. The policemen flanked them in their hi-vis jackets and stood with their hands behind their backs. As Bunter approached, his new trainers scrunching on the gravel, he gave them a wide grin and a thumbs up gesture.

'Got to keep fit to deliver what the public want,' he wheezed.

'Mr Bunter, can you tell us about the Russia report?'

'How did she get here?' muttered Bunter, recognising the reporter he had knocked over with the excavator. He waved at her. 'Yes,' he said, 'Thank you!' he called out.

'But Mr Bunter...' by which time Bunter was sliding into the walnut and leather opulence of a Range Rover.

'That bloody woman,' he said.

'If you need somebody to take care of her, boss, just say the word,' said the driver.

'Good lord. I didn't mean—no, not at all. Not at all. Even so,' he clenched his fist, 'bloody woman.'

Chapter Thirteen

KAMINSKY REACHED RAJMAR Pandit on the third attempt.

'This is the Home Secretary. What is it?' she snapped, suspicious and breathless. There seemed to be a lot of shouting and bumping and rustling in the background. Kaminsky threw a dart at the wall where it landed between the official photos of Pandit and Cherry wearing official government smiles.

'Are you listening to the Today programme, Rajmar?' he said. 'Where are you?'

'I'm with a special operations police raid. We got the bastards.'

Kaminsky held the phone away from his head for an instant. 'What?'

'Wait. They're breaking down another door.'

'This can't wait. Bunter is on the Today programme right now.'

Kaminsky turned to his computer screen. The interviewer was saying: 'So the Northern Ireland question is resolved?'

'Absolutely, Bess. And I'll tell you this…'

Kaminsky cursed.

'I'm out here making the streets safe to sleep in at night. Nothing's more important than that,' said Pandit.

'And do we want people sleeping in the streets?'

'You know what I meant!' she bellowed, and Kaminsky held the phone away from his ear again.

'Just listen to the radio,' said Kaminsky.

He surveyed his neat office and straightened the line of pencils on his desk. Bunter was impossible to manage. Nobody had told him about the Radio 4 interview until it was too late. What was the point in being a Special Advisor to the Prime Minister if there was nothing special to advise on?

Closeted in a BBC studio Bunter folded one plump leg over another to reveal his colourful, odd socks. He had disposed of three BBC iced buns and was contemplating ordering a fourth.

An earnest looking Beth Goodenstern leaned towards the microphone: 'But won't the cost of such a project be prohibitive.'

'Oh, I'll have the Department run all the numbers of course—as one responsibly should do—but it's unlikely to cost much more than HS2 might eventually end up costing. In fact, I've seen estimates of as little as £300 billion, Bess—and I think that would be incredible value for the British taxpayer.'

'Uhm it's Beth, actually, Prime Minister.'

'So sorry,' said Bunter. 'Incredible value for the British taxpayer, Beth.' he repeated.

'£300 billion is an extraordinary amount of money.'

'All of my advice is that it will pay for itself.'

A lengthy pause ensued while Beth shuffled though some notes. Finding nothing of use she looked up. 'Are you sure?'

'Of course I'm sure, my dear. Nothing surer. The government doesn't go about willy-nilly embarking on major infrastructure projects like this without absolute certainty of a return on investment. And what's more it solves the border issues with Northern Ireland at a stroke. We had a Professor from Liverpool University look at the feasibility of this project as long ago as last year, you know. He proposed a road and rail crossing between Port Patrick, in Dumfries and Galloway, and Larne in Northern Ireland. And Treasury has been beavering away at the maths ever since. We don't just dream these things up overnight, you know Bess.'

'Beth,' responded Beth with a sharp intonation.

'Indeed,' said Bunter, nodding blissfully.

'You know, this is quite unexpected. I haven't had time to do the research,' said Beth, floundering.

'It's quite OK, Bess. I understand you invited me here to talk about some mythical plans for an election, and not the most important priority in government at the moment. Which is getting Brexit done. And this bridge,' he said, prodding the table with a forefinger, 'is a big chunk of the jigsaw.'

'Well, I'll … I'm sure we'll have you back here to discuss this exciting development in more detail.

'Of course you will,' said Bunter, winking, and hugely enjoying himself. 'And I feel sure that next time you'll be much better prepared.'

The LBC studios were rather better appointed than those of the BBC, but there were no buns, just a few dry biscuits and a mug of instant coffee. Nick Ferrari flashed him a predatory smile. A girl patted Bunter's face with a powder puff. He tried to pull in his chair and it wouldn't budge, so he leaned down and fiddled around, looking for the obstruction.

'It doesn't move,' said Ferrari with a smug look.

'Why on earth not? It always used to move.'

It's bolted to the floor. We call it the Bunter Bolt.'

Bunter laughed. 'Bunter Bolt? What's that all about, then? What a beastly trick.'

'It's because whenever you're interviewed on here and the questions are not to your liking, you seem to slip off camera.'

'I say, that's most unfair. And untrue,' blustered Bunter.

'Two minutes,' said somebody.

'Now, surely we can unfasten this chair?' said Bunter, wriggling. 'You've had your fun.'

Ferrari shook his head and Bunter folded his arms. 'Good morning Prime Minister,' said Ferrari with an evil smile. 'I listened carefully to your interview on the Today programme a short while ago. Can you tell our listeners more about the Northern Ireland solution that you're proposing?'

Bunter put back his head, ranging his gaze around the ceiling. 'Well it's not yet a proposal, or course,' he said.

'Are you backtracking now?'

Bunter looked directly at the camera with a mischievous look. 'Good lord no! It's just not the way we do things in government. I don't just come on air making vague proposals.'

'So what's changed?' said Ferrari. 'Because in my experience that's exactly what you do.'

'Oh come on, Nick. You've got me here on the spot. Bolted to the spot, in fact. That's a most unfair accusation.'

'So tell the listeners about the Bridge.'

'Well, it's the most exciting prospect—but of course it hasn't been debated in Parliament, and you know Nick I have the most enormous respect for parliamentary procedures. However, what I can tell you— how I saw it, when I conceived the idea—is that this will act as an umbilical cord for Northern Ireland, fastening it irrevocably to the mainland and ensuring it is an integral part of this United Kingdom. We'll call it the Brexit Crossing.'

'And what work have you done to assess its feasibility from a purely construction perspective.'

'Well Nick, I've looked at what the Russians did in Crimea…'

'You mean their invasion?'

'No, no. Of course not. But what I was referring to—what I meant was—the bridge. The Russians built the Crimean Bridge. The Kerch Bridge. The longest in Europe at over 19 kilometres. And look—it's nothing new. It's been evaluated many times in the past. The last time was by Professor Dunlop at Liverpool University.'

'So it's not your idea at all?'

'The public doesn't care whose idea it is. The public wants to know justifiably whether it will address the last remaining Brexit issue—that of Northern Ireland. And I think it might.'

'So, this is your last ditch bid to make Brexit work?'

'Nick, as you know there are many solutions on the table. Many solutions to address the political status of Northern Ireland. This is simply another option that government is evaluating. And we'll put our best engineering brains on it, as we've done since the time of Balfour and beyond, Use our legendary British ingenuity, and carry out all the due diligence one would expect and emerge with the best of all possible worlds.'

'And if it doesn't stack up? If this is not the answer? What's your next best solution to a border in Northern Ireland.'

Bunter leaned across the desk, glancing at the camera. 'There will be no border between the UK and Northern Ireland. Over my dead body.' He thumped the table for emphasis. 'You have the word of this Prime Minster.'

'Well thank you for that clarification, Prime Minister. I'm afraid that's all we've got time for. Except for one thing…'

'Anything, Nick. Ask me anything.' He beamed.

'What is happening with the Russia Report?'

Bunter sat back in his chair and laid his palms on the table. 'Well you know I'd like to answer that question, I really would, Nick. But the answer, unfortunately, is not mine to give. I've no influence at all on the publication of the Russia Report, and what's more I don't know what's in it. And if I did I couldn't tell you. And anyway whatever's in it, it won't be much of anything, I can assure you of that.

'But here's what the public wants to know—I'd like to tell you what the public would like to know, Nick—and that's not whether there was spurious meddling in the Brexit referendum by the KGB, but when can we get Brexit done and when can they start to benefit from all the initiatives that Brexit will allow? And the public wants to know that I'm working hard to do just that, Nick.' Bunter turned to camera and made a thumbs up gesture. 'I'm Getting Brexit Done.'

Chapter Fourteen

THE RED-BRICK SPIRES and crenelations of Greyfriars School overlooked the rugby fields with hubris, and the sun glared down upon the clipped and crisply lined grass, where the entire school was assembled for a charity rugby match, followed by a prize-giving presented by that most famous Greyfriars Old Boy of all, the Prime Minister of the United Kingdom, William G Bunter.

Bunter was a cause celebre, hailed by teaching staff and students alike, accompanied by the frilled, powdered, and pampered Marianne, his future bride. Hands were grasped and shoulders patted, and drinks and food and treats of all kind were thrust upon him. He found it difficult to maintain a serious expression, a whisper of a smile ever present. Who would have thought it? William G Bunter, welcomed as a celebrity at his own school? He's show them. He'd show them all, including Lord Mauleverer who was the other speaker for the event, sipping beside him at a flute of champagne with a sleepy demeanour that gave him a perverse look of superiority. It seemed to Bunter to be a peculiar trait of the aristocracy and one that he tried hard to emulate. He tried out a wearisome sigh.

The lower Third were putting on a desultory display of rugby on the hard pitch, plodding without enthusiasm from end to end and devoid of tackles and contact of any kind. It seemed to be the modern way in schools.

'A course in my day rugby was a messy affair,' attested Bunter to an elite group of minor celebrities and teaching staff. The teachers looked much younger than he remembered. 'A more physical game entirely. When we played, we tackled hard and boys got hurt. It could be beastly.'

'Were you in the First XV?' enquired a pimply faced man with freckles and round glasses who had clearly never ventured onto the pitch himself.

'Nearly,' said Bunter, sipping at his champagne. 'I think the chaps will remember me as something of an, ah, phenomenon on the rugger pitch.'

'Why don't you get out there and show 'em, Bunter?' drawled Lord Mauleverer in a drowsy voice. 'Show 'em some real rugger, like we used to play on this very field.' He gestured towards the field with his glass and seemed to wink at somebody over Bunter's shoulder. Bunter remembered that Lord Mauleverer had in fact been a rare phenomenon at rugby, Captain at one time of the First XV.

'Gosh, I wouldn't want to show anyone up,' said Bunter.

'Oh go on, Billy,' prompted Marianne. 'Show them what you're made of!'

'Yes do,' said Growfinch, the headmaster, who to Bunter's eye looked like an intern in spite of an incongruous handlebar moustache. 'We'd love to see you demonstrate your sporting prowess in front of the school.'

'Oh, I don't know,' Bunter mumbled into his glass.

'I'd like to see that,' said a very pretty woman with a pinched nose and high cheekbones. Bunter thought she looked East European. She was taller by a couple of inches than him he estimated, and was slim and rounded at the same time in a pleated, printed summery dress. 'I'd like it very much.'

'Very well,' said Bunter, newly invigorated and feeling the adrenalin rising, 'I shall,' he said with decision, and to a small patter of applause he removed his jacket. He thought he saw Lord Mauleverer exchange a knowing glance with Growfinch, before he was almost bodily propelled onto the sports field by a small scrum of dignitaries. Then somebody blew a whistle and the juniors formed up for a set piece, just as a huddle of photographers assumed on the touchline and aimed their lenses. It was like Greyfriars circa 1976— even the sun was shining bright. Except that in 1976 he would more than likely be found in the tuck shop and not on any sports field. Marianne was clapping with delight and calling his name.

He drew a deep breath, steeling himself. He had hated rugger at school. In shirtsleeves and long trousers Bunter lumbered onto the field to join the scrum, which on the piping of the whistle quickly collapsed under his weight, with juvenile legs and limbs floundering. From the touchlines Bunter heard the rousing cries as the ball broke free, whisked up by the scrum half of the opposing team. Bunter gave chase at once, on the heels of a small, lithe Japanese boy who was sprinting down the field. His heart pounded and his legs were shaky, but he kept pace for at least fifty metres before launching himself upon the small boy, burying him and the ball beneath twenty stone of manly blubber. What a feat! The crowd gasped and whinnied and a man in a white coat rushed onto the field. Bunter stood up raising the ball aloft in victory, but crowd was silent and the boy didn't stir at all. The man in the white coat was bending over the boy, sponging his forehead. The pitch had become still and subdued. The spectators were quiet, except for the whirr of camera shutters, and some mumbles.

'Is he alright?' said Bunter. 'It wasn't my fault, y'know.' He looked over to Marianne who was shaking her head in despair. 'It wasn't my fault,' he called, 'I barely touched the lad.' He looked down and the boy seemed to be recovering, sitting up, or at least hunched over. The medic shot him an accusatory glance.

'He'll survive.'

'It wasn't my fault,' repeated Bunter. 'He shouldn't have—I mean if he hadn't stopped so suddenly…' the medic didn't answer. The boy coughed. 'I'm the Prime Minister, you know,' said Bunter in a defensive voice.

Chapter Fifteen

AS THE GIANT black Mercedes swept through the streets of Luxembourg, Bunter was feeling wheezy and weary after a stupendous lunch with the European Commissioner that had begun shortly after breakfast. He liked to think he had given a jolly good account of himself on behalf of the British people and was prepared to tell the EU that Britons would never ever be slaves. He liked that turn of phrase and whipped out an old parking ticket from his pocket to make a scrawled note of the words with a gnarled Bic on the back of the envelope. Might even use it at the press conference to which he was heading now, alongside that upstart the Prime Minister of Luxembourg with the Greek name he could never remember. What was needed, he mused, was an ultimatum. The car slowed as a few protestors with placards strayed from the pavement.

'What's going on? Who are these people?'

'Rabble, sir. I will not let them obstruct us.'

Bunter frowned. 'Do I detect a Russian accent?'

'I am from Minsk. Why do you ask?'

'It just seems strange that everyone around me seems to be Russian these days.'

'Russia is big. Bigger than any nation on earth. Bigger even than British Empire once was. It is not surprising that our citizens are to be found throughout the world.'

'I suppose not.' Somebody slapped the bonnet of the car, and the car nudged the protestor aside, creeping forwards, it's engine almost silent. 'What are they protesting about?'

'You,' said the driver.

'Me?'

The driver gestured out of the window. 'It's what their banners are saying.'

Bunter looked. An elderly man in a 'T' shirt thrust a cardboard placard at his window that said: 'Bog Off Bunter.' A waving banner carried the words 'IKEA has better cabinets.'

'What in blazes has got into them?'

'I think they have emotional attachment to EU. It was the same with Soviet Union. Nobody knew what happened with those activists. Except us.'

'Us?'

'Security services.'

Bunter grunted. 'Is there anything to eat in this car?'

'Of course. There is refrigerator between seats.'

Bunter opened the compartment and found a selection of sandwiches. He closed it. 'No muffins or buns?'

'We will be there shortly.'

'I'm beginning to have second thoughts.'

A firecracker fizzed over the car leaving a trail of smoke.

'There is no cause for concern. This car is bullet proof. And you have *krisha*.'

'What the devil is *Krisha*?'

The driver gave a sharp laugh. 'It's what we say in Russian. Protection. Like Mafia, yes?'

'Well say what you mean in English. And the British government is not to be compared with the Russian Mafia.'

'That's true. It is not so organised as organised crime.'

'Did we get you from an agency?'

'Almost, sir. The Agency is our competition.' Bunter's eyes widened. 'Mr Ignatov wished to make sure that you are in safe hands.'

'Well you can tell Mr Ignatov from me that we have our own people for that. And what's more … what are they doing now?' A string of protestors in blue shirts ringed with golden stars had joined hands across the road obstructing Bunter's car. They were shouting 'Bollocks to Brexit'.

'Don't worry. This is why they hire me,' and the car ploughed through the crowd at a sedate crawl, leaving behind a confused disarray. People were picking themselves up from the street.

'You could have jolly well hurt somebody,' said Bunter in horror. 'Some of them might even have been British.'

'They were all British,' said the driver with a careless shrug. 'That's how I knew they would yield.'

Bunter was uneasy. He jabbed at his phone and Kaminsky picked up at once. 'There's a big protest going on in Luxembourg,' he said.

'It's not so big,' said Kaminsky.

'My driver ploughed through hundreds of them.'

'Twenty or thirty,' said the driver over his shoulder. 'Nothing compared to old days in Moscow.'

Bunter threw the driver his sternest look. 'They're planning to stage the press conference outside. D'you think it'll be safe? Can't we get them to do it inside?' he said into the phone.

'I've already asked on your behalf. They refused—I think they're enjoying the prospect.'

'It's only the Prime Minister of Luxembourg. It's not even a proper country. I thought it was fly shit on the map.'

'I wouldn't use that expression in public, Billy.'

'Well, it's outrageous. Here am I, the Prime Minister of Great Britain being held to ransom by the smallest country in Europe.'

'The best you can hope for is rain,' said Kaminsky, untroubled.

'The best I can do is not turn up,' grumbled Bunter.

'You're right!' said Kaminsky with sudden enthusiasm. 'That's the answer. Leave them with an empty podium. There's no better demonstration of Britain's attitude to Europe. Why didn't I think of that?'

'It would mean missing the buffet,' said Bunter with reluctance, hunger gnawing at him as it usually did.

'The RAF will feed you on the flight home.'

'I hate military grub. And there's never any fizz. What this country needs is a Prime-ministerial jet with proper catering. Like my chum Fisher T Fisher has in America. We could call it the Brexit Jet. Don't you have any chums in the airline business? Didn't you used to own an airline?'

'It didn't get off the ground,' said Kaminsky. 'It was from my Russia days.'

'You don't talk much about those days.'

'No, I don't.'

An awkward pause before Bunter asked without much interest: 'Anything happening at home I should be aware of?'

'It's raining again,' said Kaminsky, and rang off.

❖

The Cabinet meeting the following day was all bluster and rancour.

'As I see it,' Bunter was declaring, 'this is our chance to make a scene. To give those unelected bureaucrats in Brussels an ultimatum.

This is our turning-on-the-heel moment, where we walk out of the debating chamber in a fearsome huff. I must say I feel personally slighted,' said Bunter with genuine affront.

'It was an insult, Prime Minister,' said Pandit, nodding with solemn righteousness.

'A calculated one,' said Truscott, grim-faced and indignant.

'The insultingness has never been greater,' said Singh.

'What? Eh?' said Dutton.

'I think it's rather jolly,' said Cherry with a laugh, brandishing a copy of The Guardian. The front page displayed a photograph of the Prime-Minister of Luxembourg surrounded by the flags of the EU nations, addressing an empty podium where Bunter should have been. 'It says here: "It would take the strength of the comic hero The Incredible Hulk, to leave the EU with a deal". That's what they think. Didn't you tell the press we were making "big progress"?'

'That was me,' said Truscott. 'I thought we were, but I've not been to Brussels much. I've left it to the negotiating team.'

Bunter looked at Truscott with hooded eyes. 'And who exactly is the negotiating team? Aren't you supposed to be our Brexit Minister, old man?'

'Well, yes, but you can't expect me to do all the negotiating. I'd be hoarse, old boy.'

'Get Brexit Done,' said Dutton with a quiet thump on the table.

'Shut up, Dutton,' said Bunter.

'Eh, what?' returned Dutton with a newly awoken expression.

'Could we get The Incredible Hulk?' asked Cherry with insouciance.

'That's not helpful,' said Bunter.

'I loved this turn of phrase,' pursued Cherry in undisguised hilarity: 'From Incredible Hulk to Incredible Sulk,' he said, jabbing at the text.

Kaminsky coughed from a corner of the room where he habitually observed the Cabinet meetings. 'I agree with the Prime-Minister. We should be viewing this as an opportunity to press for a no-deal.'

'And is that what we want?' said Cherry.

'It's what we've wanted all along,' replied Kaminsky.

Chapter Sixteen

'YOU LIED, BUNTER!' echoed a baritone voice through the corridors of Westminster. 'You lied to the Queen.' Heads turned. Jaws dropped.

'I didn't. I wasn't. It wasn't my fault.,' stammered Bunter. 'I wasn't even there.'

Quelch advanced down the corridor like an invading army.

'You are even more insidious and deceitful than you were as a boy, Bunter. I know your father! I've a good mind to give you a good spanking right here and now!'

Bunter looked about him in horror. 'Now look here…' he began.

Quelch planted himself in front of Bunter, his sharp beak only inches from Bunter's plump face. 'I know what you're up to Bunter. I've heard all about it. At best what you've told Her Majesty is misleading … at worst it's treason! Treason, y'hear, boy?'

'I'm not a boy. I'm the Prime Minister.'

'You'll always be a disobedient boy to me, Bunter.'

'It was necessary, sir. I mean, my lord. It was vital to prorogue parliament at this point. That's what I was advised. What I was told. They made me do it, in fact.'

'Stop stammering boy. Have you any idea of the penalty for treason?'

'I don't. I mean it wasn't. It was necessary, don't you see?'

Quelch looked horrified. 'Necessary, boy? Treason?' he barked.

'No, no. Not treason of course,' stammered Bunter. 'The proroguing of Parliament. In order to deliver our agenda, doncha see? We have—I mean it's the Domestic Abuse Bill. It will be set out in our legislative agenda.'

'What piffle is this? If you prorogue Parliament it'll be dropped along with all the other bills. And why don't you return my calls? I've been calling and calling. I was on hold for two hours one time.'

'Calls, sir? I didn't have any calls. No messages. Not one. Not from you, my Lord. I've been awfully busy, you know. But I would've known. If you'd called, that is.'

Quelch put a heavy arm around Bunter's shoulders and steered him along the corridor, leaning down to speak. 'I want to know what's happening about my report.'

'Your report, sir? What report would that be.'

'You know very well what report, Bunter. The Russia Report.'

'Ah, yes. That report.'

'Why hasn't it been published?'

'I've seen an early draft, sir.'

'It's damning. The whole Brexit shenanigans—all influenced by the Russians.'

'I don't think it goes quite that far, sir.'

'Are you calling me a liar?'

'No. Well of course not. But the Russia Report—from what I've seen—doesn't say very much at all. And that's absolutely the truth, sir.'

'Then publish it. Let the nation see,' said Quelch, making a fist and squinting at Bunter with one eye half closed.

'It's not my fault, sir. I mean to say, it's not my decision. It'll be published in due course. When the time is right. But I can't interfere. It's nothing to do with me.'

'I think it's everything to do with you, Bunter. You and your cohort. Where does this Kaminsky character come from? What was he doing in Russia all those years? Isn't he your fag or something? Your SPUD?'

'SPAD, sir. Special Advisor. He's from Yorkshire. He was delivering British expertise to Russia to help them build a new airline. As fine an example of our entrepreneurial spirit as you'll find anywhere. I vouch for him personally.'

'As a voucher Bunter you've no more value than a Green Shield stamp.'

'I promise you, sir. I give you my word as an Old Greyfriarian. That report will be published. I'll personally make sure of it, if I have any influence. Which of course I don't.'

'See that you do,' grumbled Quelch, removing his arm and setting Bunter free at last.

'How's the book coming along, sir? The History of Greyfriars?'

'Still a work in progress, my boy. Just editing volume eighteen.'

'Can't wait to read it sir. I really must go, now. And I didn't lie to the Queen. Honest I didn't, sir.'

'I'm watching you, Bunter,' Quelch said, wagging a half-hearted finger.

In a hurry to escape his Greyfriars nemesis, Bunter stepped outside the Parliament building and the sky was overcast: it looked like rain again.

❖

'How did you get in here, Skinner? Are you even a member?' said Bunter, quite horrified, from his regular table in a quiet corner of the Carlton Club's Macmillan Bar. It was a Wednesday or a Thursday, Bunter couldn't quite remember which, and he had sought refuge away from the eyes of Westminster, Quelsh particularly and Marianne's frightful mood. A bottle of claret on the table was either half empty or half full, and a single dog-eared crust was all that remained of a sumptuous afternoon tea for two. A hawkeyed waiter hovered in a morning suit nearby in the a pale sunlight admitted from the terrace windows that imparted the mahogany bar with a yellow glow. A pleasant aroma of beeswax filled the air. At the bar a Conservative MP with wild eyebrows whose name Bunter couldn't recall was busy trying to stay upright.

'Don't let them near you,' he was counselling a young intern in a polyester suit. 'I'm not like that, y'know, but there are plenty that are, d'you see?'

Harold Skinner's eyes darted left and right. He had the haunted look of a fugitive. 'I've got to talk to you, Bunter old man. There's no one else I can trust.' Skinner had been the least savoury of all the pupils at Greyfriars and ran a notorious gambling ring under the noses of the teachers.

'Would you care for a glass of wine, dear fellow?'

'Not here,' said Skinner. 'I'll take a large scotch on the terrace.'

Bunter summoned the waiter, helped himself to a large glass of wine, and then escorted Skinner out onto the terrace.

'What the blazes is it, old chap?'

'They're everywhere,' said Skinner. 'Everywhere I go. They hacked my phone, too.'

'Who did, old man?' said Bunter with concern.

'Journalists,' spat Skinner. 'I shook 'em off in Cleveland Row earlier. I don't think they'll follow me in here.'

They seated themselves at an iron table on the terrace. There was a gentle, bracing breeze. The waiter brought Skinner's drink and he swallowed it in one and ordered another.

'Why are these journalists following you?' said Bunter.

'I can't say too much about that, if you see what I mean.'

'Something illegal?'

'It may very well be,' said Skinner, averting his eyes. 'Look, old man, are you going to help me, or what?'

'But you haven't said what you want me to do!'

'I want him hurt,' said Skinner with bitterness. 'I want him not to be able to get out of bed. The principal journalist – his name's Coleman. He works for the News of the World.'

'Oh lor,' said Bunter, signalling to the waiter. 'I'll have the same as him,' he said. He lowered his voice: 'I'm not sure that's the kind of thing one does. I mean I am Prime Minister and everything, you know. Somewhat in the public eye, if you see the problem.'

Skinner saw the problem. 'But you're the most powerful man in the land,' he said, 'God knows how, but you are. You must be able to do something. They're plaguing me, outside my apartment with their long lenses. Following me in the street.'

'But what do they hope to find?'

'I had some debts. You know what it's like old man. Some gambling debts. I had to raise some money fast.'

'Bunter's jaw was lolling open. 'So what did you do?'

'Nobody was meant to know. It was quite innocent.'

'So what was it?'

Skinner sighed and pecked at his empty whisky tumble. He breathed in the fumes. I think I need another one of these,' he said.

The waiter was already at Bunter's shoulder. 'Two more, please,' he said without taking his eyes from Skinner.

'It was a jewel heist,' said Skinner. Bunter's eyes widened and he looked swiftly around the empty bar. 'Not a real one. Just for—well, you know the insurance. The police were never involved,' he hastened. '…and it all turned out well in the end. Pops loaned me what I needed and everyone was happy. Except somehow this journalist found out.'

'So what are you going to do?'

'I want his address. I want to track him down. Do him some harm.'

'But what can I do?'

'Can't you get me his address or something? Don't you know anyone in your position?'

Bunter suddenly thought of the offer from the Russian driver who had offered to perform a similar favour in respect of a journalist. 'What exactly do you want to happen to this man?'

'I want to warn him off. Send him down with a couple of black eyes. Nothing too serious. I don't want to kill him. Not yet.'

'What does that mean?' said Bunter, 'Not yet?'

'Not ever. Not really. Just to frighten him. Let him know I'm not to be messed with.'

Bunter found that he was enjoying the prospect of demonstrating his power and knowledge. 'Well as it happens, I might know just the man.'

'You, Bunter?'

'Surprising as it may seem I have my underground connections.'

❖

Bunter ordered an official car to take him home from the Carlton Club, and when a prim lady wearing pince-nez and a dark suit nudged his elbow to inform his that his car had arrived he was nodding off in an armchair. He looked around for Skinner but he was nowhere to be seen, just the same half-familiar vague-limbed MP at the bar, edging closer to a male intern.

'So sorry,' mumbled Bunter. 'Must have dropped off. Pressures of high office.' He stumbled to his feet and went out into the empty street. Early in the morning, he reminded himself he was heading up to Scotland in the much-hated RAF jet to meet with the US President. At the kerb waited a glossy black Range Rover, and his driver from Regents Park opened the rear door.

'Good to see you, uhm…?'

'Dmitry,' said the driver, pushing the door to as he nestled inside. 'Downing Street?'

'Drive around a little first,' said Bunter, 'I was hoping it would be you.'

'You have something you wish me to pass on?'

'Pass on? No, I don't think so. Where would you pass it if I did? Never mind all that. It's about what you said. About taking care of somebody. Not in a good way.'

Dmitry drove with calm authority, the headlamps sweeping over rows of stuccoed Georgian houses. Bunter wondered when it had got dark. 'This journalist, I think,' said Dmitry, 'The woman. Something you want us to do with her, yes?'

'Yes. No … no. Not her. I'm not asking for myself. Not something I could personally contemplate. Couldn't live with it. Not for me, but for a friend, you see. An old school friend.' He found himself almost whispering even though there was nobody to hear.

Dmitry turned back and gave a sly wink. 'I understand, Prime Minister.'

'No, no. I don't think you do. It really has nothing to do with me. Honestly. I need to make that very clear.'

'Clear and understood. You speak on behalf of friend.'

'Yes, that's it. A school chum, in fact.'

'You want us to hit schoolboy?'

'Not a schoolboy. We were schoolboys together. A long time ago. In school.'

'I get it.'

A rumble of tyres while Bunter considered. 'You just said the word hit.'

'Yes. You wish us to make hit on this schoolboy for your friend, yes? We call this wet job in KGB.'

Bunter sat up straight. 'Crikey, no. Not a hit job or a wet job. And not a schoolboy. I think we may be at cross purposes.'

'Please tell me Mr Bunter name of person that you wish for us to eliminate.'

'Not eliminate either. Gosh. I hope you don't think… what I want is—what my friend wants—I think he just needs roughing up. Maybe a couple of black eyes. That sort of thing. No worse injuries than you would pick up on the rugby pitch.'

'We can accommodate this. Please to write down name.'

Bunter wrote the name on the back of another unpaid parking ticket he had been carrying around for weeks and handed it to the driver. 'Please don't kill him.'

'I will tell them be gentle,' said Dmitry. 'Would you like to go home now?'

'Yes please. Early start tomorrow. So when will you do this—this job?'

'This is not something I carry out personally, you understand. But soon I think.'

'Only tomorrow I'm in Scotland.'

'This we know,' said the driver with a knowing look. 'and here is your stop.'

'Thanks awfully,' said Bunter, stepping into Downing Street.

Chapter Seventeen

'HERE IT IS, pal—the most anticipated golf tournament in history—use one of these.' And the President thrust a driver at Bunter, who looked at the length of wood and steel dumfounded, the rain streaming down his cheeks.

'Is this the right tool, old chap?'

'No, it's you that's a right tool,' said Fisher, assuming the phoney vowels of an English accent and chuckling. His umbrella bearers, tall bulky men in matching waterproofs, burst into unjustified merriment at this witticism and almost allowed a stray droplet to descend on Fisher's immaculate, slick coiffure.

Bunter did not have an umbrella bearer and fumbled to juggle between the golf club and the umbrella. His spiked shoes squelched in the rain-sodden turf and sucked at his feet, and he felt miserable. They stood upon a small hillock, overlooking a lengthy decline to a patch of sodden sand and a red flag. The rain blew in horizontal layers across the course and all of it seemed to end up in Bunter's face. A bluish camera flash ignited from a few metres away.

'When you suggested a golfing tournament, I rather expected you meant at your Camelot resort in Florida,' said Bunter without grace. 'In the sunshine. And not in Scotland. Have you any idea how I manged to avoid the First Minister?'

'Pussy,' said the bone dry and crisply attired President. 'You're supposed to be like, you know, 'Fisher Lite'. Don't be a wimp—smash the ball into outer space. I don't want you to give me a bad rep. Not when I had the New York Times and Fox News shipped out here to record this event.

Bunter lay his umbrella down in the mud, took the long shaft in both hands, lining up over the ball, like he'd been instructed only a week ago on a dry, manicured slope in Surrey.

'The hole's that way,' said Fisher, gesturing with a laugh, and his aides snorted. One of the two men raised a beefy arm, revealing the butt of a pistol, as though to pat Fisher manfully on the shoulder, but Fisher glared at him, and parity was restored. The rain pattered on the presidential umbrellas.

Bunter made infinitesimal adjustments to his stance before presenting the club squarely, once, twice, and then snatching the shaft back and forth in a graceful arch, connecting with the ball at last and sending it hopping across the turf to settle a few feet away.

'You can take that agin,' drawled the President with a smirk.

'I'd rather not, old bean. Fair do's. A slip of the avuncular bone in the swing.'

The President shot him a suspicious look, sighting him with one eagle eye. He hated for anyone to even think they had got one over him. He levelled the head of his club towards Bunter.

'You should—you can get creams for that condition,' he said, and bent his back into his shot, muttering 'maybe not in Great Britain, though. Maybe use bleach instead.' Then he swung his club and hit the ball with a resonant crack. 'Would you look at that,' he said, shading his eyes against a non-existent sun. 'Into the beyond. Is that a hole in one? It might be. It's a mystical thing.'

A distant figure sprinted across the green and seemed to deposit a ball in the hole, before skittering away.

'Bunter squinted through the downpour. 'Didn't I see …? Wasn't there somebody …?'

'Well wouldn't you know it,' said the President, shouldering his club. 'A hole in one,' he said, shaking his head in apparent wonder.

'But there was…'

'What?' snapped the President.

'Oh, never mind. Well played of course. Jolly good show.'

A gust of rain laden wind hit Bunter in the face, and he wiped his mouth dry on the back of his hand. Fisher stalked off through the sodden grass, and Bunter trailed behind deep in misery. 'When you proposed a golf tournament, Fisher old chap, I rather thought you meant at your Florida resort.'

'Just call me by my Christian name,' retorted Fisher T Fisher over his shoulder.

'But I thought … I mean I assumed…'

'Get's 'em every time,' laughed Fisher to his aides, who gave a synchronised holler of mirth. One dared to give the President a gentle punch in the arm.

'Oh,' said Bunter, 'I see,' his face contorting in a mirthless smile. 'Very funny, Fisher old man.' He was hobbling now, and his chest was heaving. 'About this trade deal, Fisher. I know you said we would be first in line…'

'The very first, William. William the First of England, you might say.'

'Wasn't he a Norman?'

'Nope, he was definitely a William, said Fisher and this time one of the President's aides slapped him on his back and hooted.

'Definitely a William!' repeated the aide with another guffaw.

'Yes, yes, said Bunter, ignoring the laughter, 'but I had hoped…'

The President turned around and raised up his chiselled (dry) chin, resting his hands on the handle of his club. 'Fisher T Fisher is a man of his word,' he pronounced. 'We will have the mother of all trade deals. It will be big and exciting and truly majestic.' He glanced at the press huddle and seemed to address himself now to the reporters. 'In the future, let me tell you, we're going to be very involved with the UK. I mean, you don't hear the word Britain anymore. It's very interesting. It's like, nope.' He shook his head in mystery. 'It'll be a big trade deal – much, much more business than we do right now, many, many times. I think the EU has been an obstacle to trade, very, very protectionist, and very unfair,' he paused as flashes blinked in the gloomy light, and then held up a protesting hand. 'That's all I have for you folks,' he said with a chuckle, then he turned back to Bunter and beckoned to him. 'C'mon William. Let's smash these balls off the course,' and wielding his club like a cheerleader's baton he led Bunter into the driving rain beneath the shelter of his own mobile canopy.

'The next hole is a hum dinger.,' said the President, surveying the bleak landscape below them, umbrellas buffeted by wind. 'It's a par 5, but you won't do it in that.'

'I don't see the green at all,' said Bunter, screwing up his eyes against the rain.'

'The fairway cuts away behind that rocky incline.'

'I see,' said Bunter, not seeing.

'But there's a sand trap.'

'There would be.'

Fisher lined himself up over the tee and made intricate movements with his feet.

'About this trade deal, old chap.'

Fisher put up a cautionary hand. 'Don't distract me.' He made a few passes at the ball, then hauled back the club and hit the ball somewhere out of sight. 'Would ya look at that baby go,' he said.

'I can't see it at all,' said Bunter.

'That's because it's curved around the prominence there and onto the green,' said Fisher.

As an accomplished cheat himself, Bunter recognised the simplicity and elegance of Fisher's cheating, but it didn't make him feel any better. The President's aides high-fived each other without losing their grip on the umbrellas.

'Follow that,' said Fisher, and Bunter did, directly into the rough, 10 metres away.

'Can we talk about the trade deal?' said Bunter with impatience. 'I've promised…'

'As a successful businessman, a multi-billionaire, I learnt an important lesson early in my career. Always have focus.'

'I thought your father left you his media empire?'

Fisher threw him a sour look. 'That aside,' he said. 'Always focus. That's been my lesson. Even wrote a best-selling book about it. The Importance of Focus. And right now my focus is on the golf. Let's go find your ball.' And the President trod off with Bunter behind.

'Are we going to eat something soon?' said Bunter. 'Only my doctor said I should consume more calories.'

After Bunter had dried out and changed, the two world leaders were to be found bowed over their steaks at a secluded table in a cavernous dining hall overlooked by the heads of stuffed animals, the walls hung with tartan rugs, stabbing at their unappetising steaks with their steely knives. A log fire spat and blazed in a huge slate-built fireplace, while security men with buzz cuts dressed for the office occupied tables at a discreet distance, nursing bottles of Fisher branded mineral water.

'So have you met with the Ruskies yet?' mumbled Fisher to his plate.

'Sorry, what did you say?'

Fisher looked at him with a shrewd eye. 'The Ruskies. Did you meet with them yet?'

'Should I have?'

'President Putin called me up personally to congratulate me on winning the election,' said Fisher, chewing his steak. 'We have deep respect for one other. As leaders. I think that's an asset.' He spiked another piece of meat. 'So did you? Did you meet with them?'

'I… well, it's a matter of secrecy. State secrecy. But between the two of us—that is you and I—not directly. Not yet. Although I expect to meet with him in the new year.'

'Don't let them piss on you,' said Fisher. 'That's all I'm saying. It won't go well for you if you do.' He pointed his fork at Bunter. 'You know what I mean.'

'I'm not sure I follow, old chap.'

'The girls. He'll set you up if he can.'

'I don't… I mean I've never.' Bunter was trying to remember what happened exactly in Umbria. 'I mean do you think he would, actually?'

'Not to me. Although I did stay at the Moscow Ritz-Carlton that one time. That's the only grain of truth. There is no pee tape. I can say that without any word of a lie.'

'I never thought there was, old man. You don't need to convince me.'

'There isn't. I swear it. And if there had been, the CIA would have destroyed it.'

'I did go to a party once, where there were girls. You know, Russian girls.' reflected Bunter with an ominous feeling.

'That's how it starts. That's how they get you. A party. Broads. Professionals, if you see what I mean. But don't believe everything you read in the New York Times.'

'I most assuredly won't,' affirmed Bunter. 'I don't mean to pester, but can we talk now about the trade deal?'

Fisher sat back in his chair and assessed Bunter. 'I'll tell you quite frankly, William. I feel we've got something. Something here,' he made a meaty fist and punched his chest where his heart should be. 'Like we're cast from the same metal.'

'I think so too,' said Bunter. 'I've always thought that.'

'You're not like those others that come to me, begging for favours. Not like that woman—what would her name have been?'

'May,' said Bunter.

The President chuckled and corrected himself. 'What MAY her name have been? You Brits and your grammar...' he flapped a hand. 'It doesn't matter what her name may have been. You're different, and as a result—as a reward—I'm prepared to cut you a deal,' concluded Fisher with a wide grin.

'That's wonderful,' said Bunter, feeling a genuine warmth sweep over him. 'Is there dessert?' he ventured.

'I'm gonna start you off with lamb.'

'For dessert?'

'No, no. Not dessert. I mean I'm prepared to lift the embargo on British lamb.'

'I have to confess, old chap—I didn't know there was one. An embargo, I mean.' Bunter gulped a mouthful of Merlot, held the glass up to the light and gulped some more. 'This is really rather splendid.'

'It wasn't my fault about the embargo. I've always thought it was unfair. Goes back centuries for all I know. Predates my presidency in any case. But we can start there. Waddya think?' Fisher looked at Bunter with a critical eye.

'And do Americans eat a lot of lamb?'

Fisher laughed. 'Barely any at all,' he said, 'but that's not the issue.'

'And what is the issue?' asked Bunter, reasonably.

Fisher laid his cutlery down on his empty plate.

'Incremental steps,' said the President. 'That's what's called for here.'

'Slowly, slowly catchy monkey?'

'What?'

'Just a … never mind, old man. Forget I said anything.'

Fisher appeared nonplussed but continued: 'We wouldn't want anyone to think there was any favouritism going on. For example, the French. The French are so jealous. So, so jealous. Anyhow,' he said, making mediating gestures with his hands, 'we take it nice and slow at first. Incremental steps. Meanwhile we negotiate the biggest free trade deal the world has ever seen. Bigger than all the trade that's ever done through the WTO. A beautiful trade deal. And we hit 'em with it right between the eyes. Splat!'

Bunter started when Fisher slapped his palm on the table. He spluttered: 'I, of course. I concur. That sounds like a most excellent plan, Fisher. Most excellent indeed.' He raised his glass in salute. 'Here's to lamb. And did you … I mean was there any prospect of dessert d'you think?'

❖

'Incremental steps?' said Gloria Pendlesham on a call later.

'Indeed,' confirmed Bunter. 'Isn't that an admirable outcome?'

'I'm not sure what it means if I'm honest, Prime Minister.'

'Well look, after some tough negotiating the President has agreed to lift the US embargo on lamb after simply decades. You can tell the press that. We took a tough stance on this, I can jolly well tell you. I was most forthright, I don't mind saying. This is a big day for British sheep farmers.'

'But Americans don't eat much lamb, do they?' said Gloria in a dubious tone, 'I remember when I was at Disneyland Florida with the kids it was impossible to find a good lamb chop anywhere.'

'That's really not the point,' hissed Bunter.

'What is the point, Prime Minister?'

'It's an incremental step. That's the point, in a nutshell. Along the road to a beautiful trade deal of immense proportions. We've embarked on our new negotiating strategy with the US, something that was impossible before Brexit. Incremental steps. I think Fisher used those exact same words. We're making history here, Gloria.'

'So you want me to issue a press release to that effect? Making history and everything? New negotiating strategy? Incremental steps? Blah, blah?'

'Exactly. But don't bother with the Guardian. Just send it to the usual suspects. And be sure to mention that only Brexit has made this possible. Clear?'

'Yes, I think so. Only Brexit has made this possible. When are you coming back?'

'Is it raining there?'

'Do you have to ask?'

'Well then I may need to stay a little longer dear girl, just to cement this deal.'

Chapter Eighteen

KAMINSKY BUTTONHOLED BUNTER in the Member's Tea Room at Westminster presiding over a table loaded with pastries. He was sitting at his customary table in a quiet corner of the oak panelled room, the white table cloth scattered with crumbs and stains. There was a buzz of discreet conversation. Across the room Dutton was dozing over a pot of tea.

'They're going to let you have it,' said Kaminsky drawing up a seat uninvited.

'That's rather unchivalrous,' said Bunter, his cheeks swollen with food. 'It wasn't my fault, you know.'

Kaminsky looked puzzled. 'What wasn't your fault?'

'Whatever reason they have for letting me have it.'

Kaminsky sighed. Sometimes it was hard to be a Special Advisor. I mean they're going to let you have your way. Our way, in fact.'

'You should have one of these chocolate croissants, you know,' said Bunter, pointing to a plate. 'What way is that, old chap? What way are they letting me have?'

'I had a quite word with Stella McTrouton and Julian Barnsley-Thorpe, and they've agreed to back your election.'

'Should I know them?'

'The leaders of the SNP and the Liberal Democrats. With the DUP it will give us the two-thirds majority we need to swing it.'

'These leaders change so often. It's hard to keep track.'

'We've have a few leadership changes ourselves,' reminded Kaminsky.

'Ah but not any more!' said Bunter. 'Now the Conservative Party has got what it always needed. Somebody that will navigate the slings and arrows of outrageous fortunes. To dodge them.'

'They've always needed somebody dodgy.'

'Indeed,' said Bunter as his phone vibrated on the table. He picked it up.

'Who's this?' he snapped in irritation.

'Here is Volk.'

'Wolf, old chap, 'what a pleasure to hear from you,' said Bunter, pointing at the phone for Kaminsky's benefit and mouthing the word 'Ignatov'.

'Your phone is being monitored so I will be brief.'

'I don't think so, dear boy. Nobody would dare to bug the phone of the Prime Minister.'

'I guarantee it. We have laughed over of your exchanges many times.'

'I say.'

'So I have some news. Firstly there will be election.'

'Yes, Kaminsky here just told me.'

'He did. Yes. It will be on twelfth of December. Also we have taken care of that other business for you.'

'Other business? I don't follow.'

'You gave assignment to your driver?'

'Oh, erm… yes I suppose I did.'

'It is complete. Also we make another job. Two for one,' he chuckled.

'Another job?'

'Of course. As friend it is minimum I can do.'

'Well thank you. My friend will be very grateful. I'm in your debt.'

'Yes,' said Volk, 'you are. Goodbye.'

After the line went dead, Bunter wondered for a moment about the 'other job', but only for a moment.

'How does Volk know about the date of the election?' said Bunter. 'I don't even know that myself.'

'I was about to tell you.'

'A bit rum, I must say,' grumbled Bunter. 'I'm not nearly prepared.'

'You don't need to prepare, Billy. We have everything in hand. In fact, where possible stay away from the hustings. Just perform a few clownish events, you know the kind of thing.'

'Clownish?' he blinked. 'Me?'

'I hear you're seeing your old buddy Herbert Tudor Vernon-Smith this afternoon?'

'And what of it?'

'It's a good idea. We should use him. He'll be anxious to make amends.'

Bunter's phone trembled and buzzed. 'Can't a fellow have a bit of peace while he's eating?' He swiped the phone and answered. 'Skinner, dear boy. What a pleasure.'

'What did you do, Bunter? What have you done?'

'What?'

'He's in hospital. He can't walk.'

'Who is? You're not making much sense.'

'Coleman. The journalist. I didn't mean you to… just a couple of black eyes, I said.'

'It wasn't me. I wasn't even there. You can't just blame a fellow…'

'I asked you to help. But this…' Skinner trailed off with an incoherent sob.

'But it wasn't me, I tell you. A couple of black eyes, that's all I would have told them. If I told them anything—which I didn't.'

'Now they'll really be out to get me, won't they? I'll never forgive you for this, Bunter,' said Skinner.

'But I was trying to help. You said…' but Skinner had ended the call. Bunter thought with discomfort about the other journalist who had been plaguing him.

'Problems?' said Kaminsky, without much interest.

'Nothing a chap can't handle,' said Bunter, picking up the last chocolate croissant and feeding it into his mouth.

Later at an office in Chelsea Bunter greeted Herbert Tudor Vernon-Smith with a cry of: 'Crikey—would you ever?—it's The Bounder!' and gripped him in an unwelcome embrace. 'Delighted to see you old fellow.'

The Bounder as he had once been known to Greyfriars pupils, extracted himself with some distaste. He was the stylish antithesis to Bunter, immaculately dressed in a tailored suit of impeccable taste matched with a sober necktie. He was tall and slim and had movie-star good looks.

'Careful, old boy. Don't crumple the yarn.'

Bunter pumped his hand instead. The Bounder's office was appointed in the plush manner of the Carlton Club, and carried the same aroma of beeswax.

'Take a pew,' said The Bounder, ushering Bunter to a capacious recliner.

'I have to apologise, said Bunter, leaning his rear into the cushions. 'for all that unpleasantness after the Brexit campaign. It wasn't my fault y'know.'

The Bounder flapped a slender hand. 'No need, old chap We're all grown-ups, aren't we?'

'You did a sterling job old chap—although I don't pretend to understand it all. Positively sterling. With all that Facebook data you stole, I mean.'

'We acquired all of that data on commercial terms, I'll have you know. It's a pity we had to close down the shop,' said The Bounder. 'But the result has never been in question, and for that we should be thankful.'

'Oxford Analytics was a superb example of British ingenuity,' said Bunter. 'A flagship of the digital economy.'

'I suppose it was,' said The Bounder, settling himself behind his desk. On the wall behind him were framed pictures of The Bounder with various heads of state, including Paul Kagami, President of Rwanda and Viktor Yanukovych, former President of Ukraine. Affability was The Bounder's main positive attribute, and he exuded it in every handshake.

'But now we have TES—The Election Shop. Tailor made results, that's our slogan. We're working with President Lukashenko and Viktor Orban at present.'

'And that's why you're exactly the right man to talk to about my election campaign. And the fact that we were at school together gives even more credibility.'

The Bounder seemed to consider this at length. 'After the unfair and spurious allegations levelled at Oxford Analytics—not to mention the fines—d'you still think I'm the man for the job, old man? I wouldn't want to cause you any kind of bother.'

'I don't think we need to worry about that. You weren't to blame, after all. What do you think you could do for me?'

The Bounder considered, presenting a perfect profile to Bunter as he stroked his chin. 'I think we should firstly set out to play the man and not the ball.'

Bunter looked puzzled. 'What's that supposed to mean?'

'In my experience many politicians are too squeamish about personal attacks. There's lots of flannel about fair play and Queensbury rules, whereas in reality they're quietly thrusting stilettos in each other's solar plexuses. Or should that be solar plexi?' mused The Bounder.

'As a classics scholar I can affirm that I haven't the faintest idea. Plexi or plexus is equally good by me.'

'Solar plexi, then,' he corrected himself, 'But you're different, Bunter. I remember from school that you were always admirably lacking in scruples.'

Bunter beamed. 'Thank you.'

'So here's what I propose. Firstly we leak a lot of tosh on social media and the press about the Leader of the Opposition's links to the Zionists. Or conversely to Hamas. Perhaps we keep our options open and leak both. Maybe we should let it be known that Brian Beaver is a Holocaust denier?'

'Is he?'

'Of course not.'

'Anything else?'

'Sexual scandals are usually a safe bet, or at least they used to be. We could send some girls around to Beaver's house. If the wife's at home, so much the better.' said The Bounder, 'Maybe bring some Ukrainians in on holiday with us, you know what I'm saying… I find that works very well.'

'Sounds perfectly feasible to me. I must say I'm shocked to learn of this other dimension to Beaver's character,' said Bunter with mock gravitas.

'Then we can call into question the finances of the Labour Party. Shouldn't be too tricky if we can find a few dodgy union donors— they're all Marxists, and the mere scent of Marx or Hegel drives the voters into a paroxysm. Or maybe Hamas is a better bet these days? So we have a sexual deviant whose party is funded by international terrorists.'

'That's sure to get the voters rattled,' said Bunter with glee.

'What's the endgame, Bunter? I mean what's in it for you? There's not much dosh in being world leader and I never saw you as an altruist.'

'I just think it's the biggest ever prank. Just think of it—Billy Bunter, the actual Prime Minister.'

'I see what you mean,' said The Bounder.

Chapter Nineteen

As BUNTER ENTERED the apartment at Number 11 he was ambushed in the living room by Marianne and a florid woman who seemed to be displaying the contents of an entire English garden on her dress, and was as gushing as a garden hose, reaching out with a dramatic gesture to welcome him home.

'This,' announced Marianne with enthusiasm, 'is Wendy Hauss.'

'Wendy House,' repeated Bunter feeling that the irony of the name had not been given full weight.

'Call me Wen, Prime Minister,' gushed Wendy Hauss. 'Everyone does.'

Bunter opened the cocktail cabinet where he helped himself to a large cognac. He also grabbed a handful of almonds. 'Delighted, dear lady,' said Bunter in a tone that suggested he was anything but delighted.

'You have a wonderful home,' said Wendy with a prim smile. 'But if you'll forgive me—it does look rather like a gentleman's club.'

'I like gentleman's clubs,' said Bunter who had visited a few and intended to go on visiting them.

'Not the kind of clubs you mean,' said Marianne.

'I don't know what you're talking about,' said Bunter.

Wendy clapped her hands. 'Now, to work!' She said.

'Hi ho, hi ho,' muttered Bunter.

'Wen will help us to restore some taste to Number 11 after that dreadful woman.'

'When?'

'Yes Wen. Wendy Hauss.'

'No, I meant when will she perform this miracle?'

Both women looked puzzled. 'Instantly,' said Marianne.

'I can start right away,' said Wendy.

'And who is going to pay for it?'

'Oh, I'm sure you'll find somebody to do that,' said Marianne, trailing a hand on the arm of the despised sofa from John Lewis. 'Wen has some magical ideas.'

Wendy's eye flitted around. 'I thought a floral theme,' she said, to nobody's surprise. She had a rolled-up sample which she unfurled for Bunter to see. 'Just look at this. Isn't it simply divine?'

What Bunter saw was a riot of golden curls and cornices in relief against a scarlet background. He shrugged.

'Do you see the effect Wen is striving for?' said Marianne

'All I see is a roll of wallpaper,' said Bunter.

'Just visualise it,' said Marianne, her eyes glazed as she stared around the innocuous plain walls.

'It's 24 carat gold leaf,' added Wendy.

A draught of cognac caught in Bunter's throat, and he spluttered and coughed. 'It's ah, very nice indeed, Wen. Extraordinary in fact,' he said, catching Marianne's fierce expression just in time. 'Quite extraordinary.' Wendy and Marianne floated around the apartment pointing at walls and furniture with Bunter in tow. 'So how much is this wallpaper?' inquired Bunter. 'You know, just for illustrative purposes?'

Wendy flashed him a smile. 'I'm sure I can get the price down below £800.'

'That sounds reasonable,' said Bunter with relief.

'Each roll is unique, hand crafted,' said Wendy, leaving Bunter with an ominous, unsettled feeling. 'So, anything below £1,000 a roll is amazing value.'

'Wen is interior designer to the stars,' said Marianne.

'Per roll,' repeated Bunter, feeling quite sick.

'Are you really sure about this, Piglet?' said Bunter much later at Marianne's bijoux apartment in Chelsea, having consumed his customary two bottles of merlot with dinner. 'I mean all this wallpaper and wainscotting nonsense? And that dreadful woman, Hector Haus or whatever her name is?'

'Wendy. Wendy Haus, and she's very nice,' said Marianne. 'She designed Elton John's home.'

'Piglet, I'm not some piano playing super star. I'm just a lowly Prime Minister on a Prime Minister's salary, struggling to cover my tuck bill.'

'Then you better find somebody to pay for this makeover because I refuse to live in an apartment furnished by a middle-class department store,' she pouted.

'Piglet…' Bunter remonstrated.

'No, really Billy.'

Bunter shifted his corpulent frame across the sofa and tried to entwine himself around Marianne in a gesture of inexpert and dubious romance.

'Get off me you oaf,' yelled Marianne, pushing him away. 'Get off!'

Bunter backed off, lifting a glass of wine from an elegant Georgian coffee table. 'I'm—look. Let's start again, old girl,' he stammered.

'And I'm not your old girl,' she said with a fierce expression.

Bunter angled a meaty elbow to take a draught of wine and somehow missed his face, which was not in the place he had left it. The wine flowed in a minor torrent onto the carpet and the sofa and there was an ominous silence as both watched the red stain creep over the rose embroidered cushions with horror.

'You did this!' shouted Marianne at last, leaping to her feet. 'You destroyed my sofa! You just don't care for anything because you're spoilt. You have no care for money or anything. You're just a buffoon!'

'I say, old thing,' said Bunter, struggling to extract himself from the sofa. 'I say.'

'And I'm not an old thing,' she yelled, throwing a book at Bunter, which missed and thumped against the wall.

Bunter shielded himself with both hands. 'Look Piglet, I…'

'Get out of my fucking flat,' she thundered.

Chapter Twenty

SO HERE THEY are: the doorsteps of Britain,' said Bunter, scanning a row of modest detached houses with Georgian facades. 'The British hinterland. The red wall.'

'Oxborough & Ripestone has had a comfortable Conservative majority since the constituency was formed. Not much of a red wall,' said Sir Michael Winterford, Chairman of the local Conservative Party, with a prickly edge. He wore a tweed jacket and cavalry moustaches, and what looked like a Winchester school tie.

'Even so,' said Bunter, 'I must prevail against the communists and the anarchists everywhere.'

'Not many of those in Oxborough and Ripestone, either.' said Winterford. 'No communists under beds. Not that I've seen.' He gave a startling harumph at this.

'Get Brexit Done,' said Bunter giving a thumbs up and his most winning smile.

'You don't need to convince me,' said Winterford. His eyes were deep set and red rimmed, like he had spent the entire previous evening in the Conservative club bar, which indeed he had. 'Nor those buggers for that matter. They all want Brexit around here, so they say. Pushing at an open door,' he said with another loud harumph.

Acacia Avenue was an avenue lined not with acacias but with cherry trees, which were on the whole more decorative, at least in the spring. Currently the avenue was also lined with police officers and pressmen who were there to give a candid record of the Prime Minister's constituency canvassing. They had put in place police roadblocks at each end of the street and there was a helicopter buzzing in the air to encourage particular candour, authenticity and fair play. There was therefore no traffic, so it was authentic to the degree that the nineteenth century was authentic.

'*Fléctere si néqueo súperos Acheronta movebo,*' pronounced Bunter at the threshold. Winterford gave him a blank look. 'If I cannot bend the will of heaven, I will raise hell.' Winterford continued to regard him without comprehension. 'It's Virgil,' explained Bunter in equal incomprehension.

'If I were you, I wouldn't do too much of that in Oxborough and Ripestone. They're not used to foreign languages spoken here.'

Bunter was indignant. 'But it's not a foreign language. It's Latin! We spent hours at Greyfriars copying down this stuff.'

'For punishment?'

'Well, yes. Mostly,' admitted Bunter.

'Then I wouldn't try to punish the voters, if I were you.' Winterford nodded to an immaculate paved pathway with a wicket fence bordering a neatly clipped lawn. There was a discreet wooden sign at the gate that said: 'Welcome Prime Minister.' The TV cameras bobbed closely behind and Winterford said to the cameramen: 'Try not to get the sign in the picture, would you? Otherwise I'll be accused of cheating. Orchestrating tame interviews.'

'I say, you haven't have you?' said Bunter.

'Of course I have. Have you any idea what ordinary people here are really like?'

Bunter reflected for a moment. 'Let's proceed,' he said, steeling himself and mussing up his hair for his 'man of the people' look.

Bunter and Winterford led the line of pressmen down the garden path and a fluffy microphone on a mast hovered over Bunter's head as he pressed the bell. The door opened at once to a middle-aged woman in a formal cocktail dress, wearing far too much rouge on her cheeks and far too much chain store jewellery. She bared her teeth at Bunter. 'What a wonderful surprise,' she said. Bunter could smell the mint toothpaste on her breath.

'Absolutely delighted. Look, I have a brochure for you,' he said, looking diffident, thrusting an election brochure on the woman and taking a step backwards. 'Can I count on your vote?'

'I've voted Conservative all my life, and so did my husband when he was still alive.'

'That's wonderful,' said Bunter.

'I think they're all out to get you, if you want my opinion,' she went on, holding the brochure in a tight fist. 'They're trying to do you down, that's what they're doing, because they're desperate to stop you. But you're too intelligent for that Beaver person and the Labour Party so they they'll resort to anything, won't they? Bless you, you don't deserve this, nobody does.' She seemed to have a tear in her eye. 'I still have faith in you, faith that you'll take us out of Europe where we'll be far better off. You really do remind me of a young Churchill.'

❖

Bunter was ushered down the path of another house, staked at intervals with boards beseeching people to 'Vote Conservative,' and displaying in each of its downstairs windows a blue poster featuring Bunter's Cheshire cat grin. A few withered lavender plants along the border made a valiant effort to prosper. Winterford stepped forward and knocked at the wood effect uPVC door, and it was tugged open at once by a dour, shabbily dressed man in carpet slippers. He had a hairline that had receded into his neckline, but tufts of curly black hair prevailed around his ears.

'Good day, my man. Can I count on your vote,' said Bunter, thrusting an election leaflet at him.

'Wait,' said the man in a gruff tone, pushing the door closed.

They waited on the doorstep for several minutes, Bunter, the camera crew and Sir Michael Winterford, shuffling their feet.

'Where do you think he's gone?' hissed Bunter at last.

Before Winterford could answer the door swept open and the man stood there again holding a sheet of A4. He put on a pair of reading glasses and cleared his throat.

'You are the best thing that happened in Oxborough, we were well happy when we got you,' he declared in an odd, monotone that carried a thick accent. 'We always liked you before but when you became our MP, it was brilliant. And then when you became Prime Minister it was even better. You always have such great ideas, and are a genuine person. Like Churchill was. The others are out to get you and that's it. Also I've heard that Labour is funded by international terrorists and its leader is a sex pest. I'm backing Billy. And he reminds me of Churchill.

A diminutive woman with an unruly perm and a pinafore peeked from behind the man's back and then disappeared.

'It was OK?' said the man, removing his spectacles.

'You can stop the filming now,' said Winterford in a weary tone.

'You're not English, are you?' said Bunter. 'Not that it matters of course,' he added. 'I'm the Prime Minister of all the country. Even if they're not English.'

'Iss obvious?' He smiled, revealing an uneven set of yellow teeth. 'Originally no. I am emigrate from Volgograd, in Russian Federation. Formerly USSR.'

'I find it incredible that I'm meeting so many Russian immigrants lately. You're a mainstay of our community, you are, and I salute you,' said Bunter, saluting.

'Thank you, sir and I wish you very luck,' said the man pushing the door closed. The woman still peered out of an adjacent window, past the grinning poster.

'Well, I think that went awfully well,' said Bunter, hoisting the waist of his trousers. 'They really do seem to like me. Do we get to eat now?'

'It's only ten o'clock, Prime Minister.'

'Excellent. Time for a snack.'

The Prime Minister's cavalcade proceeded to a local business in a business park just outside Careley Plokford. The five vehicles with police escort and flashing blue lights pulled in on the way at a branch of Dunkin' Donuts and Bunter was in the back of his Range Rover gorging on doughnuts washed down with a tin of vodka and tonic.

'These cans of plonk are a great idea,' Bunter enthused, 'but they really should make thme in pints. It could be a Brexit Benefit. I think we should work on that, what do you think, old bean?'

'It has merit,' Prime Minister, said Winterton, suggesting by his tone that the idea was entirely without merit and was probably the most ludicrous proposal he had ever heard vocalised by a Prime Minister, living or dead.

The procession pulled into the car park of a large industrial unit bearing a sign that said 'Catz Cream' and a logo that portrayed a set of cats' whiskers in pink.

'What sort of a name is that?' grumbled Bunter.

'It's a play on words,' said Winterton. 'You know, as in the cat that got the cream. The owner is called Cat—short for Catherine. Catherine Modesty.'

'But not with a 'z',' said Bunter.

Winterton sighed. 'Indeed. Not with a 'z'.'

The employees in paper hats stood in two lines to greet Bunter, leading the way to the doors of the unit. At the entrance to the unit was a small, dumpy woman who introduced herself as Cat. She had a moist handshake, and everything else about her could be described as moist.

'Welcome, Prime minster,' she flooded. 'Welcome to Catz Cream.'

The press was grouping around them, prickling with lenses and microphone booms. 'So what do you do here?' said Bunter with bemusement.

Cat gave him a look that was neither moist not friendly. 'We make cream, Prime Minister. The clue's in the name,' she laughed at her own joke. 'Catz Cream,' she said, in cased Bunter had missed it.

Bunter nodded in appreciation with the whisper of a smile and gave a thumbs up to the employees and the press. He found himself in a vast, chilly unit with jars and bottles being transported on a conveyor and allowed himself to be clothed in a white coat and trilby to pose for a photo opportunity. He took Cat's moist hand and pointed to the jars of cream as they wobbled towards a machine that fitted foil lids.

'This is Britain working,' he said to the press pack, and Cat here is exporting to.. where exactly?' he said in a cheery aside to Cat.

'Mostly to the Netherlands and Spain…' she said.

'Exporting her delicious British cream all over the world. And Brexit will open up new markets for businesses just like hers. Better markets. Better for Britain,' he said, congratulating himself on a new slogan. 'Brexit,' he laboured, 'I can promise all of you will be Better for Britain. No doubt.' The bottles clinked and the machinery whirred, and a ripple of applause broke out, led by Cat. 'And all this nonsense about extending the term, delaying Brexit beyond 31 October and delaying all of those Brexit benefits that will allow Cat here to expand her business into America and Egypt—it's not going to happen. I would rather be dead in a ditch than allow that to happen. As your Prime Minister I made a promise to you and I'll jolly well deliver it.'

'James Peters of the Guardian,' said a voice. Bunter rolled his eyes and turned to the bearded journalist. 'Will you resign if that's the only option, Prime Minster?'

'I thought I made that very clear,' blustered Bunter, 'I mean I've said I just don't want, I just don't … I really need … look the EU is costing us a billion pounds a month, it achieves absolutely nothing. What is the point of further delay?'

'Is that a yes, Prime Minister?'

'Brian Beaver will have the country eating out of the hands of Brussels. He will have the country on its knees. And ask him where his funding comes from. Ask him about that,' said Bunter, wagging a finger. 'Thank you everyone,' he said finally with a wave.

'Prime Minister,' said a woman's voice, 'I'm Penny Torton and I'm filming you for a Channel 4 podcast,' she said, and Bunter turned to recognise the very same journalist that he had failed to run over in the excavator. He was flooded with a mixture of panic and relief as he realised that at least she hadn't been nobbled by Volk's men. 'It's on the subject of Russia's influence on Brexit.'

'I'd really rather not…' he stammered 'Oh crikey.'

'Oh, for fuck's sake,' muttered Winterton, steering Bunter away from the press.

'Would you agree to take part in my podcast, Prime Minister?' pressed Penny Torton.

'Look, I say … I'll be with you in a second,' and Bunter allowed himself to be led into what looked like a giant fridge lined with bottles and jars.

'He's gone into a fridge,' said somebody, laughing.

'It's a bunker,' said another voice.'

'A Bunter Bunker,' said another in delight.

'How long can we stay in here?' said Bunter to Winterton as the door closed. There was a single florescent bulb inside that flickered and stuttered.

'Just until the security people have sorted things out,' said Winterton, seeming to hum a little to himself. Bunter wondered if he was mad.

'It's very cold,' said Bunter. He picked up one of the jars and examined its label. 'And there's nothing to eat.'

'Tomorrow I will be in Brussels…' announced Bunter to 245 empty conference chairs and an audience of 87 party members and the press. He kept a beady eye out for the troublesome woman from Channel 4. '…and you can be sure I will be taking with me the public's forthright message on the leisurely progress of Brexit. *Non desitsus, non exieris*!' he pronounced with a raised fist to blank looks all around. 'As Virgil once said,' he added in clarification. He heard Winterton harumph somewhere in cavernous town hall. 'Which means, never give up, never surrender. Which is what we won't do. I know what you loyal Conservatives are thinking,' he went on, 'when is this bugger going to win the election and Get Brexit Done. Get it over the line. Well, you've seen the polls, and I never believe the polls. Not a chance. What you'll see will be an avalanche. An avalanche of support for Brexit and for Conservative policies. My policies.' He made an embracing gesture with his arms 'our policies. All of us here. You good fellows out there.'

Bunter rambled on this way for twenty minutes and finished with 'Remember the hour is darkest before the dawn!' before raising a cautionary finger and saying 'Beware the Beaver!'

The ripple of applause that followed was polite.

A journalist stood up. 'Simon Whittington from the Guardian,' he said.

Bunter rolled his eyes. 'Good afternoon, Simon'

'Good afternoon, Prime Minister. Would you like to comment on the incident that took place at your fiancée's flat in the early hours of this morning?'

Bunter stepped back a little looking affronted. 'Incident?'

'Neighbours said there was a commotion. Shouting and banging.'

'Oh crikey. I mean it wasn't me. I wasn't even there. Where do you get this poppycock from?'

'The police were called.'

'Look, I don't think the public want to hear about that kind of thing, unless I am very much mistaken. I think what they want to hear is what my plans are for the country and our party. And for Brexit, of course which is dearest to all of our hearts. Not to mention it's none of anyone's business what I do in the privacy of my home. Or in somebody else's home. If I was there, of course, which I wasn't.'

'If the police are called to your home, it makes it everyone's business, surely. You're running for the office of Prime Minister— therefore a lot of people who admire your politics do call into question your character and I do think it's incumbent on you to answer the question, Prime Minister,' pressed the Guardian journalist.

'I'm sure most people would really rather judge my ambitions and my character and my programme by what I deliver in office, and not by some tawdry event at which I wasn't even present. Or if I was then the event didn't take place in quite the way described.'

A few jeers came from the audience. One man began to laugh so much it turned into hiccoughs. Bunter raised his hands like a conductor in an orchestra. 'Don't boo the great man!' he said with gravity.

Another journalist stood up.

'Do you think a person's private life has any bearing on their ability to be prime minister?'

'Well, I'm glad you asked me. And no, I most certainly don't. I think a person's private life should be private. Not that I have anything at all to hide. And I've tried very hard to give my answer pretty exhaustively about the event in question—at which I was not present. And I think what people want to know is whether I have the determination and the courage to deliver on the commitments that I'm making, and it will need a lot of grit right now and I think people are entitled to think about this. And there is no time for any more questions, so I'm sorry.'

This time the applause was enthusiastic. Somebody even cheered loudly as Bunter clambered from the podium with a bashful look. Some people stood up and clapped Bunter as he left the hall with a mischievous smile, trailing a small entourage that included Winterton looking unaccountably smug. On the whole Bunter judged the day as a success.

Chapter Twenty-one

'WELL, I SAY you fellows,' said Bunter, smoothing his palms on the surface of a gleaming Walnut table and beaming at the room.

'I say,' said Truscott, looking round the table. Before the assembled bureaucrats and politicians was a clutter of A4 legal pads and pencils, iPads and smartphones. There were even a few sets of coloured pens. A row of casement windows displayed a cloudless blue sky. It was a large, and airy room with sparkling white paintwork and a long, broad table lined with men and women wearing dark suits and earnest, anxious expressions.

'Well, Billy,' said Jean-Claude Boudin, steepling his fingers. He was a man of advancing years with an aquiline nose and meticulous hair. 'Do you not wish to take notes?' he said, looking at the empty space in front of Bunter and Truscott. Bunter didn't even have a writing instrument on his person.

'It's all up here, old man,' he said, tapping a temple with a forefinger. 'Never lets me down. Nothing escapes the Owl.'

'Up here,' affirmed Truscott, tapping his own temple.

'There may be intricate legal arguments,' said Boudin. 'I wouldn't want you to…'

'Doubtful,' said Bunter.

'We doubt it,' translated Truscott. The faces around the table pursed collective lips and at least one was heard to tut.

'What do you want, Billy?'

'Kind of you to offer, old chap. Do you have any cream buns? Breakfast was frightful—continental—and I've not eaten properly since lunch,' grumbled Bunter.

Boudin consulted his watch as if to confirm to himself that it was still only three in the afternoon. 'I'm not sure they'll have cream buns,' said Boudin. 'The kitchens, well at this time the kitchens—they close.'

'Anything,' said Bunter. 'I'm truly famished. Flying does that to me.'

'It's barely an hour's flight—and you arrived yesterday.'

'I'll probably starve to death. I heard about a chap who did that, once. In a meeting, he was—just like this one. His pleading for sustenance went unheeded and then …. well he expired. Just like that.' He slapped his hand on the table and a few people started.

'Hardly plausible,' said Boudin crossing to the windowsill, and looking down on an empty Brussels street. He plucked a phone from its cradle. In English he said into the phone: 'Would you kindly arrange for Mr Bunter to have some refreshment? He tells me he hasn't eaten since—would you believe?— lunchtime. I suggest it should be a platter of something. Including some pastries, but nothing too … continental.'

Boudin re-joined the table with a wry smile and seated himself with aplomb. 'So, to return to my question,' the people around the table picked up their pens again and began to write. 'What do the British want? After all, we negotiated one deal already with your predecessor.'

'Yes,' said Bunter, 'but she's not—I mean she wasn't… well it's never simple, in British politics,' he said, shaking his uncoiffured head.

Boudin sighed. 'It never is,' he agreed.

'So what we want is the same agreement,' said Bunter. Boudin's eyes widened. 'The same, but better.'

'Better,' echoed Truscott with a tough look. 'The same, but better.'

'I know we'll be able to thrash this out,' said Bunter.

'We can thrash it out,' said Truscott, folding his hands on the table and leaning forward with a predatory look.

'You'll not find us not uncooperative,' said Boudin, looking at his colleagues as they transcribed his words on legal pads, 'but we've all been here before, haven't we?' He glanced at his watch.

'I haven't,' said Bunter, 'I haven't been here before.'

'Truscott shook his head as if in agreement.' Billy's not been to Brussels,' he said. 'Not ever.'

'Well, pops was here, of course,' said Bunter. 'Not far from here. My father was a diplomat. Or a spy. I never learned the truth. WE don't talk about it in the family.'

'Billy's father was here,' said Truscott.

'Will you stop doing that?' said Bunter with suppressed fury.

'What?' said Truscott.

'Replaying everything like a— you know...' Bunter floundered, 'like a replayer!' He said with finality.

'He wants me to stop replaying things,' said Truscott.

'Yes!' said Bunter, 'Yes I bloody well do.'

'Let's get to the nub of it,' said Boudin, ignoring the spat. 'You need a deal, and we need a deal. What is going to make this work for Great Britain? We've heard all about your sovereignty. I must say I don't deny Great Britain her sovereignty, but I'm frankly sick to death of hearing about it. No nations in history have spent so much time worrying about another nation's sovereignty. Let's get Brexit done, shall we, and put it all behind us? That way we can all move on.'

Bunter looked at Boudin with a broad smile and a feeling he was on the winning foot. 'It's all about Northern Ireland.'

'It's about Northern Ireland,' said Truscott with a vigorous nod. Bunter shot him an evil look.

'I've promised there won't be a border.'

'But countries have routinely have borders,' protested Boudin, 'It's what separates them from ... well, other countries,' he said with patience. 'If Great Britain wants a divorce we can't very well keep living in the same house and sharing the same toothbrushes, can we?'

What Bunter detested most of all about Boudin was his unruffled reasonableness. 'Yes, yes old chap. But we need to see beyond the routine. We need to contemplate the untenable.'

Boudin frowned. 'What do you mean?'

'In your excellent example, we are divorcing, but that shouldn't affect my sister, should it?'

'Your sister?'

'Yes. I mean it stands to reason. My sister's been living in the same house all these years, and then suddenly we divorce and she's kicked out of house and home. Hardly fair old chap, is it?'

'Your sister being Northern Ireland?'

'Spot on! So, what we need is an agreement that she can stay whenever she wants, use the cutlery and the heating, and avail herself of the erm, of the facilities, until it's convenient for her to find her own apartment. In Chelsea or somewhere.' Bunter paused, reflecting, 'Or in Notting Hill,' he said finally, as though he had stumbled upon the missing link. He would have picked up his pencil if he had one.

Boudin raised an eyebrow. 'I take it you're not expecting us to cook her meals and wash her smalls?'

Bunter grimaced. 'I think you're stretching the analogy, old man.'

'Order! Order!' The sharp-tongued voice of the Speaker rang out.

The House was crammed on both sides of the chamber and muttering and murmuring trembled in the rafters. Iconic green leather benches lined the chamber like those that had been polished by the posteriors of the grand and the great and the nots so great in government for 300 years, and which would outlast Bunter's government. With the whisper of a smile Bunter slouched on one such bench today facing the opposition, wedged between Singh and Truscott. He drew back his jacket to better display a rotund belly that stressed the buttons of his shirt. Brian Beaver sat opposite grey and grim faced. When the House had settled Bunter took to his feet and read from a sheaf of papers that Truscott had passed him with a wink moments before.

'The Prime Minister,' introduced the Speaker with a flourish.

'Mr Speaker,' began Bunter, 'withdrawal from the European Union is a new national project that will unite this once great nation, and I'd like to emphasise at this juncture the Government's commitment to retaining Northern Ireland in the UK. The benefits of leaving the EU are quite clear to us all: it will mean that the UK can set its own standards on subjects such as the environment. And some other things too. Probably things that even I haven't thought of yet.

'The Bill before you today may seem similar to the bill proposed by the Right Honourable lady, but it's not. It's not the same at all. It's entirely different except for some of the words, and contains provisions to ensure that Northern Ireland remains at the heart of our United Kingdom family and is not cast out like some unwanted orphan to make its own way.' He made a gesture with his hand that was intended to be illustrative. 'The brand new Northern Ireland Protocol that this government has negotiated, after many, many hours of talks, will guarantee that. What we've done, you see, is replaced the wholly unworkable Back Stop with a full stop—and there you have it...' There was a buzz of affirmation. 'And Stromont—Stormont should be jolly pleased.'

'The Leader of the Opposition,' announced The Speaker.

Brian Beaver rose from his bench with a diffident air. "Thank you, Mr Speaker. I'd like to ask, can the Prime Minister confirm to the

House that there will be trade deals with other countries ready to go the moment the withdrawal bill comes into force, in order to offset the undoubted fall in the economy caused by Brexit?'

Bunter stood up again. 'Mr Speaker, I can confirm that there are simply hundreds of countries lining up to do business with this country the moment the starting gun fires and the whistle is blown. Businesses around the country are poised to benefit from the casting off the chains of EU rules and regulations. Look at straight bananas, for example.' A ripple of laughter danced around the government benches.

Beaver stood up again, and fitting a pair of heavy rimmed spectacles consulted his notes. 'Putting aside the benefits of straight bananas, can the government be more specific about the countries that will be signing free trade agreements with the United Kingdom?'

Bunter laughed. 'Well not right now, of course. Not off the top of my head,' he wagged a plump finger at Beaver, 'But unlike the Right Honourable gentleman, this government doesn't want to dam up trade. We want to tear down those dams, and declare to all comers that Britain is open for business again.'

'Could he name just one? Just one trade agreement that will be in place when we leave the EU?'

'Mr Speaker only last week I was playing golf with my good chum the President of the United States of America. They're ready to do a magnificent trade deal with us, just as soon as we are: the biggest the world has seen. Only Brexit makes this possible. And there are others. Other great nations with whom the Trade Secretary has spoken, and some with whom she hasn't yet spoken. All of them poised, poised I say, to enter into other free trade deals, you see if they don't. And Great Britain will prosper. It will prosper mightily—possibly even more mightily than it has ever done before. The public doesn't want to hear about the minutiae of those trade deals. The public wants to hear about their Brexit bonus—and believe me it will be a big fat bonus.

'So, if the Leader of the Opposition wants to support Britain—if he wants to make Britain a wealthier, happier, more prosperous place to live, and for our children to live—then he will support this Bill today, and I commend it to the House.'

The House rumbled in concord and discord. Order papers were waved in the air on both sides and a general tumult ensued. Some MPs stood up. Some sat down. Some could not quite decide and hovered over their benches hoping they wouldn't miss anything important.

'Order!' said the Speaker, 'Order!' but the order failed to materialise.

Finally, a division was called, and MPs scuttled and weaved through the lobbies waving their passes. Bunter watched the chaos with agony and delight. 'Will it pass d'you think?'

Truscott looked at him with misery in his eyes. 'Will it pass?' he echoed.

'Let's vote,' said Bunter setting off with resolve. Truscott veered to the other side. 'Where are you going?'

I thought 'Ayes' were on the right.'

'On the left,' said Bunter in a curt tone. 'We almost lost your vote.'

'It's complicated,' said Truscott, catching up.

'There're only two ways you can go, old man.'

'I've always had a problem with my left and right, ever since school.'

'Maybe you should join the Liberal Democrats,' said Bunter, nodding towards a small and sinister looking group of men and women who hadn't yet passed through either lobby and seemed to be counting the passage of voters.

'Which way do you think they'll go?'

'Anyone's guess,' said Bunter with a wild wave at Siobhan Foster who strode with a wide body and a wide, fierce mouth through the 'aye' lobby. She ignored him.

'At least the Irish are on side,' said Bunter.

Chapter Twenty-two

LESS THAN A month later, in Oxborough town hall Count Binface wearing a costume featuring a garbage can helmet and futuristic gloves and boots was singing the Star-Spangled Banner and giving a double thumbs down to the audience. Lord Buckethead was yelling something about fake news. A man in a red costume with a yellow nose known as Elmo bounced around the stage, patting other candidate on the head. There was a festive air to the occasion, waiting for the count to be complete. Bunter, wearing a new bow tie and a blue rosette was never in any doubt about the result. Marianne clung to his arm and made desultory adjustments to her hair. She was wearing a small hat, like a stylish chocolate box or a coronet. A few stray coloured balloons danced around the periphery of the hall with the dustballs and discarded raffle tickets.

The returning officer, wearing a polyester blazer and thick rimmed glasses tapped a microphone and blew into it. 'I guess this is us, chaps,' said Bunter. A short, stout man wearing a red rosette glared at him as though he's said something obscene. He hadn't spoken a word since they arrived, even when Count Binface had stooped to kiss his bald head. The Liberal Democrat spoke with passion to everyone and smelled of toothpaste and shoe polish. Bunter had a rigid smile on his face.

'The results of the Oxborough & Ripestone election.' Bawled the returning officer, sounding like a bingo caller. He read through the names of the also-rans and some received a patter of applause. Count Binface paraded himself on stage when his result was read out, with 0.1% of the vote. Then: 'Michael Betterways, 3,026; Eddie Sunderland, 18,141; William George Bunter, 25,351. I hereby declare that said William G Bunter is duly elected.'

The hall erupted with claps and cheers and camera flashes popped and flickered. There were yells and cheers and some boos. Bunter grinned, and waved, putting an arm around Marianne. 'We won, he said in a whisper in her ear contained in a kiss. And we'll win the General Election too, you see if we don't.' He was invited to the podium, where he stood for a moment, broad and round and flushed, surveying the crowd and waiting for the applause to subside.

'Well, I bet you thought you'd seen the last of me,' he began, assembling some notes at the lectern, to a few whoops and some laughter. He made a thumbs up gesture to further applause. Today he could do no wrong. 'I don't want to tempt fate, because lots of results are still coming in, but it looks awfully like I've been given a powerful new mandate to get Brexit done…' he paused for another noisy ovation. '…and not just to get Brexit done but to unite Britain and move forward as never before. To bulldoze forward. And yes, we'll recruit 50,000 more nurses and 6,000 new GPs and build 40 new hospitals. And one of those new hospitals will be right here in Oxborough and Ripestone. And a few more things I haven't even thought about yet, including that bridge. A bridge of which you have never seen the like. Not since Crimea. And I'm jolly, jolly grateful to you, to you voters out there for returning me to office to serve you. To serve you all. And I thank the police, the council, everyone who's worked all night to count for us. My fellow candidates,' The Labour candidate grimaced. 'Lord Buckethead and some others. I don't remember all their names,' he dithered, 'but they're right here behind me.' He said with a vague gesture. 'We'll deliver all of that, and we'll jolly well get Brexit done so that all of you folks can enjoy all of the exceedingly good benefits. Thank you, Oxborough & Ripestone.'

As Bunter's entourage trailed out of the town hall in triumph, Winterton tugged him by the sleeve.

'What ho, Winters,' said Bunter, 'A great day for the Conservative Party, eh?'

'How did you do it,' said Winterton, shaking his head in wonder.

'It was all about Brexit in the end, I expect.'

'104% turnout.'

'Is that good?'

'I can safely say it's unprecedented.'

The doors to the street were thrown open for Bunter. Winterton lingered inside.

'What are you suggesting?' said Bunter, feeling somehow affronted without really knowing why.

'Only that we must have had a lot of help,' said Winterton.

'I simply couldn't have achieved this without local party support. Your team has been a godsend, old chap. A godsend. I owe you a mighty debt of thanks.'

'And not only my team, I'm sure,' muttered Winterton, watching Bunter lever himself into a car with Marianne following.

❖

Bunter sat in the plush rear of the Range Rover with Marianne as it sailed down the M4 towards London with a police escort, against the flow of the Brexit queues coming the other way. Bunter munched on a Cornish pastie that they had bought from a service station on the way. It was a bright, yellow day and some drivers had set up barbecues and awnings on the tarmac. A few saluted Bunter's car as he swept by. Even in the insulated cabin Bunter heard somebody yell 'Gawd bless ya!' from the opposite carriageway. He rewarded him with a thumbs up.

As they entered the conurbation they passed a billboard bearing the election slogan 'Beware of the Beaver.' It seemed like the nation had heeded the warning. Bunter thought the beady eyed beaver in the poster looked contrite.

The cars pulled into the portico of a hotel where two men were detaching the EU flag from its mast. Bunter's party were hustled by detectives and officials into a large conference hall. On the rear wall was a giant sign reading 'The People's Government'. Kaminsky slotted in alongside him as he was directed to a room at the side.

'The numbers are coming in fast,' said Kaminsky, looking joyous. 'It's a wipe-out for Labour across the board. The word is that Beaver will resign.'

Bunter frowned and smacked his lips. 'Will there be food, old boy?'

Kaminsky stopped in astonishment, and then caught up. 'Food?'

'Something to eat. I feel like I haven't eaten since Monday.'

A laughing man with spectacles that Bunter didn't recognise pressed a flute of Champagne on him and on Marianne as they entered the room. 'Well done, sir. Well done indeed.'

Cherry was there, looking at the TV screens. He flashed Bunter a wan smile. 'Looks like you've done it, old chap. I never thought you would.'

'What's the score,' said Bunter, sweeping crumbs off his jacket and quaffing Champagne.

Marianne pointed. 'Looks like an 84 seat majority,' she said. 'We'll be able to do whatever we want,' she said in a dreamy voice.

'Whatever I want,' corrected Bunter. 'I'll be king of the world, just like I said I would be.'

Marianne punched him in the arm.

'Ugh! You beast!' he blurted.

'Billy!' she said, sharply.

Tempus-Fugitson sauntered up with an Elizabethan air, dressed as usual in a black suit and white shirt.

'What ho Bunter!' he exclaimed, raising a glass of fizz. 'Jolly good show,' he said with disinterest. 'Nothing to fear after all, just as I told you.' His sparkling wine had taken on a greyness, almost like a mushroom consommé with bubbles.

Bunter looked at him twice. 'Is that a wing collar you're wearing, Tempus?'

'One of the many benefits of the nineteenth century, Bunter. It's detachable – that means Nanny only has to wash the shirt once a week and to change the collars daily. Have they fed you yet?' he said, as though talking about an animal enclosure.

Bunter rubbed his belly. 'I must confess…' and the moment Tempus-Fugitson snapped his bony fingers a white-coated waiter materialised and led Bunter to a long table stacked with delicacies.

'Oh lor! Oh crikey,' said Bunter with bulging eyes, hardly knowing where to start. 'Well bless me!'

Marianne watched Bunter's gluttony with rising distaste and folded her arms across her chest. Tempus-Fugitson seemed to levitate to his side and inspected the banquet with haughty aversion.

'Makes you look like Chamberlain, that collar,' said Bunter, spitting crumbs and gesturing at Tempus-Fugitson. 'Look at us,' he said, tugging at his own bow tie, 'Chamberlin and Churchill, that's us.'

A familiar woman in a marquee shaped silk dress was steered through the gathering.

'Zdravsvutiye!' she said, above the chatter.

Kaminsky stepped up at once. 'Irina wanted to witness the fruition of all her investment.'

Irina Malenkova preferred a far from dainty hand adorned with a third world treasury.

'Investment?' said Bunter, taking the hand.

Volk was there too, cradling a glass. 'We have much riding on your election win, Billy.' He winked and clinked his glass against Bunter's. 'Together we make history, yes?'

'Iss good we win,' said Irina with a pearly smile. She had expensive white teeth.

'Very good indeed,' said Bunter with uncertainty.

A bulging rosy cheeked man wearing a thick gold watch chain and a blue rosette guffawed loudly. 'They've lost North Backfordshire,' he barked. 'North Backfordshire!' repeated the man in disbelief, to a ripple of affirmation.

'Another red wall seat,' explained Kaminsky to Bunter.

'Red wall…?'

'Once we had red wall in Berlin. Now all friends together,' said Volk, flashing a gold tooth. Irina nodded without comprehension and made a hapless gesture. 'Soon we will talk about building bridges.'

'With Russia?' said Bunter.

Volk frowned into his Champagne. 'With Ireland. We will together build world's longest bridge. With Russian engineering.'

Unsettled, Bunter was looking at the screens around the room, watching the numbers and seats tumble. 'They really bought it, didn't they?' he said in wonder.

'You deserve it Billy,' said Marianne, squeezing his arm with a taut smile. 'I know it's probably not the right time, but I thought I should tell you: I'm pregnant.'

Bunter took a step back. He had a wild grin on his face somewhere between horror and hubris.

'But that's … are you sure it's mine?' he blustered.

Marianne punched him hard on the arm again. 'Whose if not yours?'

'Prime Minister,' said a gaunt, sleepless aide. 'They're calling for you.'

'I… well that's wonderful,' he stammered as he was led away to a clambering, baying crowd in the main hall. 'I'm jolly—really jolly—pleased,' he called back to Marianne without much pleasure.

Volk did a Brexit thumbs up and Tempus-Fugitson touched the brim of an imaginary top hat as Bunter was guided to the stage with a phalanx of PR men.

The press had their lenses trained on the podium, inscribed with 'The Peoples' Government' as William George Bunter clambered onto the stage and took the microphone.

'Now listen up you chaps!' he began…

And the rest is history…

Printed in Great Britain
by Amazon